YOUR JOB--
WHERE TO
FIND IT, HOW
TO GET IT

YOUR JOB-- WHERE TO FIND IT, HOW TO GET IT

Leonard Corwen

ARCO PUBLISHING, INC.
NEW YORK

Published by Arco Publishing, Inc.
219 Park Avenue South, New York, N.Y. 10003

Library of Congress Cataloging in Publication Data

Corwen, Leonard.
    Your job.

    Bibliography: p. 179
    1.   Applications for positions.   I.   Title.
HF5383.C67   650.1'4   80–22251

ISBN 0–668–05129–9 (Library Edition)
ISBN 0–668–05131–0 (Paper Edition)

Printed in the United States of America

Contents

YOUR JOB-- WHERE TO FIND IT, HOW TO GET IT

Introduction

You are looking for a job because:

* your present position does not offer enough challenge.
* you don't see any long-range opportunities with your present firm.
* you hate your boss.
* your boss hates you.
* both of the above.
* you think you should be earning more money since you work harder than anyone else in your department.
* you are unhappy with what you are doing and would like to switch careers.
* you just got fired.
* your spouse just got fired.
* your parents believe in the work ethic and insist you move out.
* your landlord believes in the work ethic and insists you move out.
* your only rich relative just died and left her fortune to her cat.

Whatever your reasons, whether this is your first, fifth or final job search, you will need sympathy, encouragement, and luck—and most important, a concrete, proven program that yields the best return on the time, effort and money you invest in your campaign.

You'll get plenty of sympathy and lots of encouragement from others. The luck you'll have to make yourself. Follow the instructions in this book carefully and chances are you will wind up with a job. You have probably heard many of these instructions before and you may think that they are too simple or that you are too sophisticated to need advice. But the streets, subways, buses and unemployment offices are full of sophisticated job hunters who keep pounding the sidewalks because either they did not get good advice or they ignored it.

There is no magical formula that will guarantee your getting a job. What is here is information gained through years of experience working with the employed, the unemployed and the underemployed.

Each chapter covers a specific step on the road to a new job. Together they comprise a detailed plan which will hopefully take you from where you are now to where you want to be at the end of your job search.

You will be shown how to organize various elements into an effective campaign—how to prepare yourself mentally for the daily routine of job hunting—how to take stock of your assets and liabilities—how to prepare a resume that will get you interviews—how to conduct a direct mail campaign and tap the hidden job market—the secrets of interpreting classified advertising—how employment agencies, search firms and recruiters operate, and how to choose and use them to your advantage—how to handle the interview and get job offers—and finally, tips on salary negotiations.

A variety of sample resumes and letters to fit most circumstances are included, together with self-appraisal instructions, forms and checklists to help you put your best foot forward.

And finally, you will find in this book a list of sources of information—directories, periodicals, books and organizations—arranged in a manner to help you quickly find the occupational data you want.

1

Job Hunting
Is Full-Time Work

Job hunting, at best, is uncomfortable. At worst, it can be unbearable. You may be disappointed, disillusioned and demeaned. Your privacy may be invaded, your brain picked and your dignity bruised. You will be dissected and rejected. It could happen over and over again.

On the other hand you may be lucky, get your job quickly and be spared an overdose of despair. But—be prepared for the worst and *don't panic.*

The dictionary describes panic as "acute fear or demoralizing terror, often contagious in a group situation." It's true. The fear that panic engenders can stick out all over you. It affects your voice, your appearance and your manner in ways that may be imperceptible to you, but which personnel people can pick up on very quickly. Whenever you get hit with a rejection, remind yourself to calm down. If you're really down in the dumps, go get a cup of coffee, call your best friend or lover, or if you have a cooperative doctor, take a tranquilizer. You might even look up your horoscope. BUT KEEP GOING!

When looking for a job, there are two things you probably *do not* have. One is income and the other a place to go in the morning. The one thing you *do* have in overabundance is time. The way you handle the latter will have a strong bearing on how long it will take to get a job. In a later chapter, we will cover the subject of time, and how to utilize it to your best advantage.

 ## Make Every Minute Count

Obviously, even though you have too much time on your hands, you cannot afford to waste it. As you will see in the next chapter, even when you are doing everything you should in your job hunt, time slips by very quickly.

You must use every available minute to further your objective—to get the right job as soon as possible. Without a routine, there is a tendency to sit around a lot, hoping something will turn up. You cannot afford this luxury. There is always *something* constructive to do. So when the activity slows down and there seems to be nothing to do, start doing something anyway. Both your morale and your prospects will increase.

2

Where the Jobs Are

Let us assume that tomorrow you are going to enter the job market. Where do you begin?

There are nine basic sources of job openings described in this book, including the hidden job market, that only a minority of applicants effectively tap. This last can be the most productive resource, but only if you know how to reach it and have the tools, patience and know-how to use it. Chapter 4 will tell you more about this lucrative market and how to plug into it. Here are the nine basic sources:

1. help wanted classified advertising in newspapers.
2. help wanted advertising in trade journals and business publications.
3. positions wanted classified advertising in newspapers.
4. positions wanted classified advertising in trade journals and business magazines.
5. direct mail—the hidden job market.
6. employment agencies.
7. executive placement firms.
8. state employment services.
9. personal sources.

Use All Sources

Many writers of books and articles on job hunting have a special ax to grind. They will tell you never to use employment agencies, or not to deal with personnel departments. I have even read books that tell you to never use a resume. These restrictions are self-defeating. Some sources may turn out to be better than others for you, but how will you know unless you try them all?

It is not enough to just be aware of them. It is necessary that they all be utilized together. Unfortunately, many job-seekers use one source at a time (usually, the most obvious—classified advertising), wait until that source is exhausted, and then go on to another one, and so on down the line. If you wait until you exhaust your possibilities with each source, you will find that job-hunting is an extremely slow and unrewarding process. For instance, if you answer all of the help wanted advertising you can find, most of which appears with box numbers and requires you to mail a letter of application and resume, you will have to wait until the newspaper mails the replies to the advertiser. This can take a week or more. Then your letter is reviewed with fifty or one hundred others. If someone likes your resume you may be scheduled for an interview. This can take another couple of weeks. So by now you have used the better part of a month to wait for a response to your reply to a classified advertisement. And unfortunately, many companies disregard your resume without even notifying you of its receipt. It's bad manners, but it's done, and you keep on waiting for the letter that doesn't come. Some ads do carry the name of the company with its phone number, but you still have to wait your turn for an interview.

Having spent a month or more answering ads, you might move on to your next source of jobs—direct mail. Here, as you will see in a later chapter, even more time is consumed. You've got to do a fair amount of research to get names of the firms you want, and then you must compose and write effective letters. Given the condition of the U.S. mail today and the frantic activities of most companies, you could lose at least another three weeks to a month waiting for responses.

So you go on to source number 3, and place an ad in your local newspaper—another 2 to 4 weeks elapse, and so on. What you'll find yourself doing is mostly waiting—waiting for replies to come in the mail, waiting for the phone to ring with an invitation to an interview. However, if you go into all sources simultaneously, you'll find that things will begin to happen more quickly. For instance, while you are waiting for a response to your reply to a classified ad, you can be writing letters and sending resumes to selected firms. While they are on the way, you can register with a few of your local employment agencies. They may come up with immediate referrals. Then when you get back to your home, you may find a reply to some of the ads you answered in the mail box.

The Snowball Effect

Within a short time after you start all of these projects, if you have done everything correctly, you should be getting some results. As a matter of fact, this snowball effect can keep you pretty busy. That is all to the good. Having an inordinate amount of time on your hands is no good for either your morale or your chances.

The point is, don't depend on any single contact or action completely. It is very easy to sit back and hope that the letter you wrote to a box number or the warm reception you received at an employment agency will end in a job offer. It might, but you cannot live on hope. You have to keep building up your chances of success by exposing yourself to many avenues at the same time.

Start now. If it's Thursday, don't wait until Sunday because you think that's when the ads are more numerous. Don't wait until after the first or after the holidays or after Christmas—or after anything.

Personal Contacts

Get in touch with your friends, relatives and business acquaintances. You never know when the most unlikely contact will result in a tip or a piece of information that will lead you to a job possibility. Make calls to all the people you know. Arrange lunch dates. Don't be bashful or embarrassed to let someone know you are between jobs. There is no disgrace in being unemployed—and you've got lots of company. Almost anyone you talk to has been through the experience at some time in their lives, and they will understand.

The chapters that follow will show you how to use each of these sources to get the job you want.

3

Classified Advertising— How to Use It

The classified section of your daily newspaper provides the quickest way of finding available positions in your area.

According to a recent survey conducted by the U.S. Department of Labor, 60 percent of employers polled reported that they hired through classified advertising.

The Sunday edition usually carries the most job listings because it provides the advertiser with greater circulation. However, the serious job seeker studies the help wanted columns every day, including Saturdays.

The most productive way to read help wanted advertising is to go through the entire page, circling every ad that offers even the remotest possibility for you. Checking ads not in your occupational specialty is not a waste of time. Personnel people are not copywriters; you have to read between the lines to see what they are actually looking for. The ad may have been listed in the wrong category, or the newspaper may have dropped it in the wrong column. So, if you don't read the entire section, you might miss it.

Reading *all* of the ads also gives you the opportunity to make a study of the job market in your community. Like most other markets, the job market operates on the principle of supply and demand. If, for example, there is a shortage of accountants, you will see it reflected in the large number of accounting jobs listed. If you are an accountant, this means that your job search will be shorter, that you can afford to be more choosy and that you can negotiate your salary from a position of strength.

Conversely, if ads for your specialty are sparse, you know you have to tighten up your campaign and work harder. You cannot afford to turn anything down, and because people with your skills are plentiful, you can't be too independent in your demands. Classified advertising statistics are taken very seriously by the U.S. Department of Labor, other governmental agencies and corporations to pinpoint trends useful for present and future planning. These same statistics can help you in your career goals. A careful analysis of ads in your job field and your community can help you keep your demands in line with the market for your skills.

Cut out every ad you think worth answering—even if it has only remote possibilities (you can refine your choices later). Don't just mark them off. They should be pasted on a card or sheet of paper. This will help you to keep accurate records of every transaction you make on every ad.

How to Read Ads

Before you answer a help wanted ad, you have to learn to read one. This is not as simple as it seems. Because classified advertising is necessarily short, it has to tell a lot in a small space. Most personnel people become good ad writers through practice, but unfortunately, there are too many who write ads that are confusing. Here is an example of a good classified advertisement:

ACCOUNTANT

Leading fashion mfg. company has opportunity for accountant with 2 to 4 years experience. Must have potential for advancement to supervisory position. Degree plus some cost background. Salary $20,000 plus benefits. Box_____.

Although short, the ad gives you a clue to many important details about the company and the job. It tells you what business the firm is in—it is a "leading company," which indicates that it is large. The level of the position is shown by the amount of experience it requires, 2 to 4 years. They want someone who has supervisory potential. You can judge for yourself if you fill that bill. The ad states that a degree is necessary. If you do not have it, applying will be wasting time. You are given the starting salary. If you are looking for $30,000, don't reply to an ad that offers $20,000. You may be worth it, but when an advertiser states a salary, it is being done for a reason. The company may be operating on a limited budget, or the position is part of a structured table of organization. The job title, specifications and salary are based on established wage and salary statistics developed by the industry.

However, there is always *some* leeway—approximately 15 percent above the offered figure is usually a safe range in which to operate. Trying for more than that would probably be an exercise in futility for that particular position.

You may reply to an ad which offers considerably less than you want, *if you qualify your response.* In your covering letter, acknowledge that you are aware of the offered salary, and request that your resume be retained for future possibilities within the company. You may get an interview in spite of your requirements. If you're answering an employment agency ad, this is a good way to get your resume on file with them.

Now let us look at an advertisement that is not very good.

MANAGEMENT TRAINEE—some college. Good opportunity with service company. Available for travel. Willing to work hard. State salary requirements. Box————.

This ad is so badly written that you might not expect to see it. But unfortunately it appears far too many times. The only word that makes any sense is "trainee," which tells you that you need no experience. The rest is pure confusion. How much college is "some college?" Would you get in if you had six months? One year? Two years? "Willing to work hard" and "state salary"—the advertiser is simply taking bids. The days when one would take a job at any price just to have work are long gone, and an advertiser who throws a job open to competitive bidding is thirty years behind the times. The most important facts have been left out of the ad. What kind of company is it? What is the nature of the position? Is it sales, administration, customer relations or communications? Do not waste your time with this kind of an ad—no matter how desperate you are. Save your energy for those ads which offer better, more specific information—and which have the potential you seek.

The Cover Letter

Now that you have clipped all of the ads you are going to answer, what is the next step? Do you address an envelope, fold and insert your resume and drop it into the nearest mail box? If you do, you will waste a lot of paper, envelopes and postage. You will also have a lot of spare time to sit and ponder why you are not getting calls or letters from companies to come in for an interview.

The correct way to answer a help wanted ad after reading it over very carefully is to write a personal letter, attach it to your resume and only then drop it in the mail box.

The cover letter should be short. It has two functions. First, it provides the needed personal touch to your printed resume. Second, and most important, it directs the attention of the reader to particular portions of the resume which have special application to the requirements listed in the classified advertisement. For instance, if you are replying to an advertisement for a circulation manager with a magazine publisher, and a knowledge of electronic data processing is required, you can, in your cover letter, direct attention to that portion of your resume which details your experience in computerized circulation systems.

The cover letter also permits you to mention points that should never be included in a printed resume, such as past earnings or desired salary. The cover letter is the place to list any other helpful information such as temporary telephone numbers, your willingness to travel or relocate, and other data not listed in your resume that would be useful to the company—and helpful to you.

The cover letter should be typewritten. Using personally printed stationery can add a distinctive touch. The cost is minor, and it will enhance the appearance of your resume. Remember, with today's large circulation newspapers, every ad pulls many responses and, at first glance, one resume looks pretty much like another. Your cover letter, if done properly and attractively, is the unique packaging that sets your resume off from the others. But remember, no cutesy letters in either form or style. See pages 117–134 for samples.

Misleading Advertising

Reading and understanding classified advertising requires practice. If you have looked for a job before, you will know that you sometimes have to read between the lines to get the message.

There are also ads that are deliberately misleading. They can lead you down the garden path into wasted interviews, high pressure sales pitches and out-and-out confidence games. Here is an example:

EXECUTIVE MANAGEMENT TRAINEE— opportunity for bright recent college grad to join a major marketing organization. Outgoing personality. Customer relations and administration. Assured future. Salary: to $500 per week for right person. Box

---

Sounds great! Interesting, challenging, and a great salary for a recent graduate.

But this is probably a sales position with an insurance company, encyclopedia publisher, land-sales entrepreneur or a similar enterprise— and possibly of questionable repute. If this is what you want, fine. But keep in mind, the $500 salary is usually a come-on. They *may* pay that for a short time; then it's sink or swim on commission.

So without being too overselective, answer only those ads that give you some idea of the kind of company and at least some of the basic requirements for the position.

The Trade Press

Although your local newspaper is the handiest source of help wanted advertising, there is another source which also can be of help to you— the trade press. Every industry has its own newspapers and magazines. Most of them carry classified advertising. A thorough reading of the publication will also give you some idea of the trends in your industry, as well as other information which can be helpful in your job search.

Trade magazines can generally be found at your local library, or ordered directly from the publishers. The way to find the publications that cover your field is to go to your library and ask for the *Standard Rate and Data Directory of Business Magazines*. The index of this directory will tell you what magazines you want to see. Under each listing, you will find the publisher's name and address. Most publications will send you a sample copy free or at moderate cost—or you can use them in your library. Answer these ads the same way you would answer those in a newspaper. They are good sources of jobs. And while you are at your library, don't neglect your librarian. Many libraries have special sections with well-informed personnel and many kinds of occupational data and materials available. Most librarians will go out of their way to help you.

Self-Advertising

There is another way you can use classified advertising—by placing your own ad in the "Positions Wanted" or "Situations Wanted" columns.

The effectiveness of this method is questionable and requires a cash investment, but I believe that someone looking for a job should explore every avenue no matter how remote. If advertising in the situations column can get you one contact, it is worth it. Keep in mind, however, that you will probably receive replies from insurance companies, brokerage houses, encyclopedia publishers and other firms looking for commission salespeople. In addition, you will receive business opportunity propositions, mail-order gimmicks and other sucker bait. And probably some oddball or obscene stuff too. Since you don't know who will reply, it is always best to use a box number—which the newspaper will generally supply—and *not* your name or address. A phone number is OK, but this can lead to some crank calls.

If you are looking for an executive position or are in a professional occupation, consider using the classified columns of trade journals. These sometimes can be very effective.

The drawbacks to this type of advertising are (1) it is expensive and (2) your ad will appear from two weeks to two months after you order it, depending upon the frequency of the publication and its closing date for advertisements. When you advertise in a trade journal, you also must be very careful to remain completely anonymous. Always use the publication's box number and do not give away any information that may enable a curious reader to figure out who and where you are. In a tight industry, a good guesser may be able to identify you.

One other point about classified advertising. Newspapers and magazines protect the identity of their box numbers with the zeal of the C.I.A. However, there is a way to break the code with the use of a little subterfuge. I don't recommend this, but it is done quite frequently. Have someone you know reply to the help wanted advertisement, using a fake resume or letter that exactly fits the job requirements. Or answer the ad yourself, using an assumed name and address, but be sure you can pick up the mail. The reply will provide you with instant identification of the advertiser. If you are interested in the company, you then make your contact by phone or letter without letting them know you are aware of the advertisement, or that they even have a job available. Never indicate that you are replying to their box ad. If they find out your method of identification you will be eliminated as a job prospect *immediately*.

4

The Hidden Job Market

A recent survey estimates that out of 90 million or more jobs in the U.S., about 15 percent (14 million) or more turn over each year. Of these, 75 percent to 85 percent never get into the public eye.

They are filled without the benefit of advertising, employment agencies or recruiters. They reflect all occupations on all levels, from trainees through executives. How are these jobs filled?

(1) From within the company. When an opening occurs, most firms look to their own staff first to fill the spot.

(2) Personal contact and word of mouth. Jack Smith, vice president for corporate development of ABC Corporation, is a personal friend of Jim Jones of DEF Company. During a golf game, Jim mentions that their assistant comptroller is being let go because of a reorganization in their financial department. Jack's firm is looking to fill just such a position. Between the 8th and 9th holes, an arrangement is made for an interview. This happens frequently at business conventions, vacation resorts, cocktail parties and all sorts of affairs where executives gather.

How to Tap It

There is a way to crack this hidden job market. It takes time, a lot of homework and a moderate investment, but the results can be very satisfying. Most personnel experts and career counselors consider it one of the best methods of finding a position. Whatever the occupation or salary level you are seeking, you should explore this method in conjunction with all other activities mentioned in this book. This method is known as direct-mail promotion, and it is simply a system of sending selected individuals and firms your resume and accompanying cover letter to sell yourself as a viable addition to their staff.

The one big advantage of direct mail over the other methods of job hunting is that your material goes directly to the individual you want to reach.

The elements of a successful direct mail campaign are:

> (1) the right mailing list.
> (2) a good resume.
> (3) a well-written cover letter.

Each of these items is vital. If one element is weak, the entire effort will be weak. The key to your campaign, however, is the right mailing list. If you do not reach the right person, the most effective resume and cover letter will have little effect.

Choosing the Right Mailing List

We are a nation of list-makers. Almost every industry, business, trade, professional organization and educational institution is on some list, or published in a directory somewhere in the United States. As a matter of fact, almost every adult is on somebody's mailing list or in some directory other than the telephone book. If you own a car or property, hold any type of management position or are prominent in any way, you are probably listed in a directory at this moment.

You would be surprised to learn how much more than your name is listed. Some directories publish biographical sketches which include information about your family, your education, your work experience and your financial condition. Most of these lists and directories are available to anyone. They can be bought, borrowed or rented. Some are available in public libraries.

The same information is available to you as a list user. For example, if you want to reach all of the purchasing managers of industrial companies with an annual sales volume of 10 million dollars and more located in New York, Connecticut and New Jersey, all you need do is specify these requirements to a list supplier or look it up in a directory.

The cost of lists supplied by list brokers and suppliers depends on size and category and is priced on the basis of number of names supplied. The company will provide you with a printed list or individual labels if you wish. Usually, for an extra charge, they will type the list on your envelopes and mail them.

Your mailing list should be large enough to get tangible results. The percentage of returns in any direct mail campaign is small. It is related not only to what you are selling, but also to the quality of your list and the effectiveness of your sales literature.

On page 164 is a directory of sources, arranged by occupation, that you can use for your mail campaign.

How to Use List Sources

When you have chosen your directories, write down on a sheet of paper the name, address and telephone number of the individual you want to reach for each company you intend to contact. The person you choose should be the head of a department. For instance, if you are an accountant, you would write to the comptroller or the treasurer of the firm. If your specialty is advertising, the advertising manager would be your contact, and so on. Do not send your material to the personnel manager. Personnel people are accustomed to working within very narrow parameters and recruit for specific positions. Usually they are the last to know that a job is open. Unless you are lucky enough to hit them just when they have a job requisition that fits your background, your resume may be relegated to the nearest hold file, or worse, to the round file underneath the desk.

It is important to remember that you are not responding to an ad. You do not know if a position exists—your letter of application is unsolicited. What you are trying to do is convince someone in management that you can be an asset to the company. If the directory does not list the department head, telephone the firm. Tell the operator you want to send some material to their comptroller, ad manager, operations manager or whatever department manager you are seeking, and ask to be given the individual's name. Do not tell the operator that you are looking for a job, or you will be shunted to personnel, the result of which would be lost time, lost call. (Incidentally, when you do have a specific individual to contact, it pays to make a call to see if he or she is still there. Directories are sometimes out of date.)

When you have learned the name of the person you want, you are ready to write your cover letter.

What to Send

There is a difference of opinion as to whether the initial contact in a direct mail campaign should be by resume and letter or by letter only. Most personnel experts favor sending a resume accompanied by a short cover letter. If you do not enclose a resume, but write a separate letter in which you give a biographical description plus the highlights of your career to each name on your list, you would have to send fifty to a hundred letters. This is not only time consuming but could be expensive, especially if you are a slow typist. Needless to say, letters must be neat and error-free, with no strikeovers or sloppy erasures. Each letter should be composed to fit the individual company you are contacting. If your letter interests one of the recipients, you would be asked to send a copy of your resume anyway, so why not send it out at the beginning?

There are two categories of applicants who may find it more effective to send a letter without a resume, and they are at opposite ends of the experience and salary scale. High level executives, in the salary range of $50,000 and over, should write to either the president of the company or the executive vice president. In this case the letter should give the salient facts about your background, including the reasons you want to work for that particular company. It should not include a chronological listing of your jobs, but should, in a few short paragraphs, review your experience, education and background, concentrating on your achievements. At the end of the letter you can indicate that a detailed resume is available if requested.

At the other end of the scale, if you are a beginner just out of school, your resume will look like a thousand others. All you can really give is your name, address, phone number and education. You could fill space with gems like "Hobbies: Mountain climbing, fishing, reading and plumbing," or "Jobs held while in school: waiting on tables at Ptomaine Tom's Eatery," or "Check-out clerk at Herman's High Price Supermarket," but they don't do much for your resume.

In this instance, your letter should be addressed to a department head and not to the personnel department. It should be short, typewritten on a single page, and should present the highlights of your education, an explanation of your objectives and your personal statistics. Farther on, you will find sample letters that you can send with or without your resume.

Letters to prospective employers, whether accompanied by a resume or not, should always include your telephone number. Its omission will result in a delay in replying that can hurt you in a competitive market. The reader of your letter is not very likely to drop everything and call the secretary to dictate an invitation to you. If you list your home number and you expect to be out a lot of the time, arrange for a temporary service, or have a friend or business associate take your calls for you. While looking for a position, you should be available for immediate contact.

Never put your salary history on your resume or cover letter when using direct mail. Without knowing what is available at the company you are contacting, you are putting yourself at a disadvantage by disclosing what you are presently earning. If there is any interest you will be asked about your salary requirements when the company contacts you.

Be sure you get all names and titles correct in your letter. Nothing can irritate a person more than receiving a letter addressed with his or her name misspelled.

Do not boast in your letter. Remember, it is merely a vehicle of introduction, the main purpose of which is to call attention to your background and the accompanying resume. Make it straightforward. Do not beg for an interview. Imploring letters are not well received.

When to Send the Resume

There has been a great deal said and written about the best days to send out direct mail. Some advertising experts claim that mail should be timed so it will not be received the first or last day of the week. The theory is that mail received on Monday or Friday will not get proper attention. This may be true for mail order sales, but I don't put much faith in it when it comes to job hunting. Mail is mail. Assume it is read the day it is received. When you mail it is not important. Just get it into the hands of the postal service, with a silent prayer that it will get to the addressee within a reasonable time.

Keep a copy of each letter you send out and attach any replies received, notes on telephone conversations or interviews you get as a result of the letter, carefully noting dates, salaries and your own impressions of any contacts. You may have a great memory, but after a few weeks of job hunting, you will have too many facts and figures to juggle around in your head to keep them all straight. Use the form on page 135 to keep your records straight.

All of the replies to your letters will not be invitations to interviews. A few will be acknowledgments as a courtesy, with a promise to keep your resume in their files. Obviously, the more letters you sent out, the better your chances of producing replies. You *could* get lucky on ten letters, but the odds are against it. But whether you send out 30 or 300, be sure that every company you can possibly reach is on your mailing list.

Follow-Up

About two weeks after your initial mailing, it is a good idea to send a second letter or to telephone those individuals who did not reply to your letter and resume. A personal call is more effective, if you can get through. If you do reach the person to whom you mailed the letter, all you need do is introduce yourself, ask if your material was received and explain that you would like to stop in for an interview even though there might not be an opening. If you accomplish this, you should realize that you may be going in for little more than a talk. However, never turn down an invitation for a speculative interview, or hesitate to ask for such a meeting. Many times an executive may have an opening in mind that he will not divulge over the telephone or by letter. He would rather have a look at you first. And, even if the interview is entirely speculative, it is always useful to meet new people when you are in the job market. You never know where such a meeting can lead. You may open the door to other contacts. You can learn a lot about what is happening in this company and this industry and, as sometimes happens, if an opening does come up later, you may have an edge on it.

James C., who is now executive vice president of a major publishing firm, owes his present position to just such a contact. His last position terminated due to no fault of his own. He was in his sixth month of unemployment. Feeling extremely low, he came to me with a reply to a letter he had written a month before to the Vice President of Operations of a large corporation. The firm was in another state fifty miles away. The VP stated that although there was nothing available at this time, if James would call his secretary for an appointment, he would be willing to see him.

Jim was not inclined at this point to drive fifty miles to see a man who had warned him that nothing was available, and he asked for my opinion.

"What are you doing for the next few days?" I asked him.

He said that he only had one appointment, to see a recruiting firm, and planned to make some telephone calls.

"Do you have enough gas to go fifty miles up and fifty miles back?" I asked.

He smiled and shrugged.

"Then get in your car and see this guy. You have nothing to lose and you can spend a few hours in the country."

Jim went up to see the vice president. There was no job. However, at the end of the conversation the VP mentioned that he was attending a symposium sponsored by the American Management Association in about a week and would keep his ears open. The ending must be obvious to you by this time. There was someone at that meeting, the director of purchasing for a top book publisher located in the suburb of the very city in which Jim lived, and that person was looking for an assistant to fill a spot left vacant by a transfer. When Jim called me excitedly to tell me he'd gotten the job, I was not too surprised. I have seen similar situations before.

The Middleman in the Job Market

A third party may be used in your direct mail campaign, but only under special circumstances. An upper-level executive or someone in a very small and sensitive industry who does not want his identity known initially, may engage a friend, his attorney or his accountant to present him anonymously to preselected corporate executives. This is done with a phone call or letter whereby the applicant is very discreetly introduced as being available for a move, using no names or company affiliations. This method is not often successful. The recipient of such a letter is often reluctant to deal through a third party.

Of course, employment agencies and search firms are really third party agents, but they offer professional services. Their role in filling jobs shall be discussed in the next chapter.

Business News

Good sources of contacts for your direct mail campaign are your daily newspapers, general business magazines and trade journals. Almost every newspaper carries business news of new enterprises, promotions, new firms coming into town and new leases signed by local firms. When someone is promoted or a new executive is brought in to head a department, some reorganization usually follows. A letter to a newly promoted executive making reference to the published item usually gets a good reception. I have personally contacted many people by mail and phone to congratulate them on their promotions. In about half of the cases, the individual was not aware that the name and photo had appeared. An-nouncements of this kind are usually handled by the public relations department and the employee is not always told where or when it will appear. People are flattered when told that you noticed their name or photograph in a newspaper or magazine. (An example will be found on page 127.)

5

How to Choose and Use Employment Agencies

Employment agencies are a prime source for job openings in the United States. A cursory observation of the classified help wanted pages of almost any newspaper shows how many jobs are advertised by agencies.

There are good reasons for using the services of an agency in addition to other job sources.

(1) Agencies can often get you immediate interviews without your having to submit a resume or make prior contact with the company. This is a tremendous time saver for you.
(2) Agencies have jobs that are not advertised or listed with other sources.
(3) They can counsel you and advise you on your job-hunting campaign.
(4) They may help you revise your resume if necessary, and might even write a resume for you.
(5) They can provide you with detailed information about their client companies and the jobs they are trying to fill.
(6) They can help you prepare for the interview and give you suggestions to make it more productive.

Agency Service Is Generally Free

Most agencies receive their fees from the client companies when they fill a job. Until they fill a position, their service is free to all parties. This financial incentive to bring applicant and employer together sometimes causes agency counselors to be a bit overzealous in selling you a job that you may not want or even be qualified for, but it also gets you more interviews.

When an agency sends you out on a job, be sure you ask if the fee is paid. If not, be sure you understand the terms of your contract fully. If you sign a contract and accept a job through an agency and you are informed that the client is not paying the fee, you are legally obligated to pay a fee according to the terms of the agreement.

Even so, remember that in most states you owe nothing until you accept a position no matter how many interviews you go on. And, in the rare instance where you do pay a fee, consider it an investment for the purchase of an income-producing job.

The Function of an Agency

In order to use agencies properly and get the most out of their services, you must first understand their function. An employment agency generally is not in business primarily to find *you* a job. Its main activity is to find employees for companies who retain its services. This is where most of the misunderstandings arise.

The distinction is important. You cannot expect your agency to conduct an in-depth search on your behalf. You cannot expect them to provide more than just cursory counseling and resume services, although some counselors will make an extra effort. Since agencies derive their incomes from the firms that retain them you cannot really demand services for which you do not pay, even though you, as the applicant, are vital to their financial success.

How to Choose the Right One

A little time spent in research and investigation will turn up the agencies that can work best for you. The National Association of Personnel

Consultants, with headquarters in Washington, D.C., is a national organization of employment agencies and consultants whose members agree to abide by a code of ethics in dealing with the business community and the public. It is made up of state and local chapters with representation in all fifty states. They will make available to you a copy of their directory listing their member agencies. These are arranged by state and city and contain the names of the principals of the firm and the types of jobs it handles. Write to: The National Association of Personnel Consultants, 1012-14th Street, N.W., Washington, D.C. 20005.

Today's employment agencies are much more professional than those of a few decades ago. Besides being closely regulated by local and state laws, the NAPC has developed testing procedures for their members. Those who pass the qualifying tests use the initial CEC after their names, designating them as Certified Employment Counselors. This doesn't eliminate all the bad apples in the business any more than the title CPA, MD or JD eliminates incompetent or unethical accountants, doctors and lawyers.

This is not to say that you should only patronize those agencies who are association members. There are many good agencies that are not.

Study the Ads Carefully

A good way to choose an agency is to study the classified pages of your daily newspaper, and note the agencies that consistently advertise the kind of job you are seeking. You will notice over a period of time that certain agencies tend to specialize. There is no point in going to an agency that generally advertises for secretaries if you are a computer programmer.

Another way to choose an agency is to make direct inquiries. If you know any personnel managers or executives, check with them. Most firms have had some experience with employment agencies and can recommend good ones. Or call the personnel manager of a well-known firm in your area, and ask if you can get a recommendation for an employment agency. You will probably get the name of the one or more agencies that the firm itself does business with. Then call the agency and tell them that they were recommended to you by their client, mentioning the name of the person with whom you spoke. The agency will roll out the red carpet for you.

Do not just walk into an agency and ask to register. You will be summarily handed an application form and shunted to the counselor who is not busy at the moment. It is best to go to an agency in response to a specific ad. If you are not replying to an agency advertisement, telephone and ask to speak to the individual who specializes in your field, and make an appointment. If the counselor says she cannot see you and asks you to mail a resume, tell her you may be in the neighborhood tomorrow or the next day and you will drop it off. Then, when you do come in, the chances are that you will be seen.

Important: Don't visit an employment agency without a resume. Most agencies require that you fill out an application form, but these forms are only useful as a file reference. Many agencies do not require applications, especially for management positions. Your resume becomes your application. Leave three copies with the counselor. Although most agencies today have a copying machine, original resumes are often better to send out to prospective clients.

How to Make the Best Use of Your Agency

One of the major advantages of using an employment agency is that you have the opportunity to ask questions that you may be reluctant to ask at a company interview. You can safely inquire as to the benefits a company offers. A counselor who is doing his job should know what the client has to offer in the way of fringe benefits. You also have the advantage of being able to discuss your salary requirements and receive advice as to how much leverage you might have in salary negotiations. An employment agency can give you information about a prospective employer that you might find difficult to obtain elsewhere.

The chances of being referred out to a position while you are sitting in the agency are slim. Counselors do not like to discuss applicants with companies while the applicant is in the office. Although agencies do not like to admit it, in most cases they also have to submit resumes before their clients agree to see the applicant. It is not true that agencies eliminate the need for submitting resumes. Many firms who have excellent relationships with their agencies still request that resumes be sent in advance of a referral.

Here is a tip. If you want to get a little extra effort out of your agency, write your counselor a personal note the next day, thanking her for her time. It is almost never done and may seem like a small thing to you, but you would be surprised at the results. Most agency counselors are under a lot of pressure. They are extremely busy people who are harassed by both employers and applicants. Since their income depends to a great extent on how many placements they can make, the daily grind is often harsh. Any small courtesy, such as a thank you note, can do wonders for their egos and make friends for you.

Keep in Close Touch

The surest way to alienate an agency is to fail to report back to your counselor after an interview. Oddly enough, about fifty percent of the applicants who are referred out on interviews simply do not bother to call the agency after the interview. Your agency will, of course, be in touch with the client to find out the results of your interview, but she should have feedback from you before she does this. She needs to know if you are interested in the job. More important to you, she can give you an idea as to what the company thinks of you. Applicants who just disappear do not encourage a counselor to make further inquiries on their behalf.

Especially annoying is the applicant who gets the job she was referred to and does not call back to notify her counselor. Agency counselors do not expect you to throw rose petals at their feet. They will be happy with an acknowledgment that you are employed through their efforts. A simple thank you note would suffice. After all, the service costs you nothing. And you may need the agency again some day.

Keep in touch with your agency counselor. You owe it to yourself to get the best service you can, and the simple courtesy of a phone call or a note will help.

Use an Agency Early

Do not use an agency as a last resort after all other efforts have failed. The employment agency is an integral part of your campaign, and should be included while developing your other sources. While you are using classified advertising, direct mail and personal contacts, all of which takes time, your employment agency can be making calls on your behalf. If you are employed and have little time for outside activities, the employment agency will be your most valuable ally. The agency multiplies your own efforts.

An agency can screen jobs for you. An advertisement can give only the bare bones of the job. But an agency has all the details, duties and responsibilities of the position listed with them. You can ask all the questions you want about the company, including the salary range and the benefits. You have the opportunity of learning all you need about a company and the job by picking the brains of the agency counselor. Do not hesitate to do this. Yours are being picked for the benefit of the client.

An Agency Protects Your Identity

Arnold D. came to my office one day, looking unusually dejected. He was employed with a good firm, but was thinking about making a move and was discreetly (he thought) studying the job market by answering a few ads.

The reason for the tragic look, he explained, was that he had just been to the post office where he had deposited his resume and cover letter in response to a blind classified advertisement. As he dropped the letter into the mail slot he had the nagging feeling that the ad he had answered seemed a little familiar. This turned into a cold fear as he thought about the possibility that he was sending a letter of application to his present employer. He had visions of his boss calling to demand why he was looking for another job. The more he thought about it, the more depressed he became. As it turned out, it wasn't his company, but he'll think twice about answering another blind ad.

An employment agency can eliminate the chance, however slight, of a job applicant answering an ad placed by his own company. No counselor would refer your resume to your present employer, or endanger your current position. If you wish, you can insist that an employment agency tell you in advance the name of his client company. If the counselor does not want to do this or is bound by a promise of confidentiality, you can then withdraw your application for the job, or allow them to present it—the option is yours. You have the major advantage of hearing the name of the employer before the employer hears of you.

An Agency Saves You Time

One of the primary reasons that a company retains the services of an employment agency is to save time. They can expect faster referrals from an agency than from ads placed in newspapers or trade journals. They expect the agency to screen quickly and carefully and submit only those applicants who have most, if not all, of the necessary qualifications for the job. This works to your advantage. If you are qualified, you get the interview quickly. If you are not, you get the bad news right away and not two weeks later after letters, phone calls and fruitless interviews.

How Agencies Get Jobs

How does an agency get jobs? How do they hear of openings? Why can't you do the same thing? Job applicants have been asking that question for as long as agencies have been in business. It is really no secret, although agencies would have you believe otherwise. The same sources are available to you, and therefore you can really be your own agent. However, since agency service is generally free, I can't think why anyone would want to do it any other way. Agencies have the same resources as you—the telephone, direct mail and the newspapers. The only difference is that it is their main business; they can spend more time getting job listings. And of course, agencies are used because it is much easier for most people to have someone else sell them instead of selling themselves.

What is generally not known is that applicants like yourself are an important source of openings. The resume you leave with an agency will show every company you worked for, your jobs and responsibilities. At your interview, you will disclose more about the firms and details about your past earnings. An efficient counselor will try to find out the names of the people you worked for plus the names of personnel managers. The job you just left is of particular importance to them because it indicates a current vacancy. After you have left the agent's office, the counselor has a good source of job vacancies. Multiply this by thousands of resumes and daily interviews and you will get a good idea of the information that is readily available to alert agencies.

Another source of agency listings is company advertising. Aggressive agencies are forever studying the help wanted pages and telephoning advertisers with the story that they just happen to have some excellent candidates with just the type of background wanted. Some firms, thus contacted and anxious to fill a position, list the job with the agency. It is not uncommon to see the same position advertised by a company and several employment agencies in the same column of the newspaper.

Many agencies send their literature to box numbers listed on blind ads, hoping that the advertiser will give them the job order, and many times they do get it.

Regardless of how they get their openings, employment agencies have been a part of the American economy for over one hundred years and are used by almost every type of organization, from small businesses to vast corporations. There are about 7,500 employment agencies in the United States today, and they place millions of men and women in jobs each year.

To ignore their potentials because of the questionable practices of a small percentage is self-defeating.

6

Personal Sources

The easiest, quickest and most satisfying way to locate a job is through a personal recommendation from a friend, business associate or relative. If your father heads a multinational conglomerate and likes you, throw this book away. Otherwise, your personal sources must be researched.

Frank M., director of personnel for a large management consulting firm and a practicing psychologist, told me that one of the main obstacles unemployed people have is their reluctance to solicit the aid of friends, relatives and acquaintances, at least at the beginning of their job hunt. After they have been out of work for a long period, desperation frequently drives them to it.

He attributes this to embarrassment and fear of appearing to be a failure to people from whom respect and admiration is expected. Some job seekers do not even tell their families for a long time that they are unemployed, pretending to leave for work and returning at the same time each morning and evening.

To dismiss these feelings as foolish and self-defeating is to oversimplify the deep emotion that causes them. There is no stigma to being unemployed. All of us are faced with it during our lifetime. You should have no qualms whatsoever about seeking aid from all sources when you need it. Every contact is a potential agent for you, for each one of them has a sphere of influence that can work on your behalf.

The first thing to do is to list all of your personal contacts in the order of their potential influence in helping you to obtain a position. Include relatives, friends, business contacts, club members, lodge brothers—

anyone you have been in contact with in recent years. Your most valuable contacts can be suppliers, clients, salespeople and others you have worked with during your career. (Of course, you can't use certain contacts if you are presently employed unless you have a close personal relationship and can rely upon their discretion.) Those in sales, advertising and public relations make particularly good sources of job openings since they come into contact with people in different fields.

 ## How to Use Personal Contacts

Your approach depends upon your relationship with each individual. The informality in dealing with a close friend or relative does not go too well with a business contact. With any contact, however, avoid allowing yourself to show self-pity. You are not asking for charity, and don't make it look or sound as though you are. If you allow desperation to creep into your voice or writing, it will embarrass them, and probably turn them away from you.

In dealing with business associates and contacts made on previous jobs, there are three distinct reactions that come into play. The first is one of sincere concern and sympathy. The second is flattery—at being selected to help a fellow human in distress. The third comes after a certain amount of time has passed—and that is discomfort, especially when your calls become more frequent and they are in no position to assist you. The discomfort can quickly turn into distaste and invariably leads to avoidance. So you have only a certain amount of time to use this type of contact. On pages 124–126 you will find illustrations of letters that are appropriate for these sources.

A word of caution. Do not tell anyone in your present firm that you are looking for a job. If you can't afford to lose your job while looking for another, keep your mouth shut. The grapevine in an office flourishes on information given and received in "strict confidence."

After you have gotten the job you want, do not forget all of those people whose help you asked. Regardless of whether they gave a lot of help, very little or none at all, send a short thank-you note of appreciation. It makes you look good and keeps the door open for the future. And for the person who was instrumental in getting you your new position, a dinner at a good restaurant, tickets to a show or a tasteful gift is definitely in order.

7

Executive Search and Placement Firms

Although the ultimate goal is the same—matching jobs with people—there are important differences between search firms and employment agencies.

Search firms work in higher salary level positions, usually over $30,000, and most search firms are geared to the $45,000 and up range. Unlike employment agencies that work on a contingency basis, earning a fee only if and when they fill a position, search firms are paid a fee for their services whether or not they find a candidate for the firm that hired them. Applicants, of course, are not charged fees. Obviously, a search firm cannot stay in business too long if they get a reputation for collecting fees from firms and not delivering suitable candidates.

Executive search firms recruit their candidates through directories, personal contact and advertising. Prospective applicants may receive a telephone call at their office or home. The approach is often indirect, with the prospect being asked if he or she can recommend someone for a particular position. If the prospect is interested, he will call back for further information.

This is a very common method of moving executives from one company to another and it is very effective. For this reason, search firms have been labelled with such terms of endearment as head hunters, pirates, flesh peddlers and body snatchers, as well as other terms not as printable.

If you are an executive you are probably already on some search firm's list even though you never wrote a revised resume or thought of looking for a job.

Executive search firms do not actively recruit to fill their files. When they receive a specific assignment they go after the person they want. They almost never place people who are not already employed.

Still, if you are an executive between jobs or are presently employed but ready to move, I would recommend that you select about half a dozen search firms and send your resume to them with a covering letter indicating your job objectives, your salary history and requirements and any other information you think would be helpful. You may or may not receive an acknowledgment, depending upon how busy the firm is at the time, but there is a chance that they may just have an opening in their files that may fit your background and requirements.

Not all executive placement firms are engaged in searches (receiving fees from companies whether or not a job is filled). A large percentage work on a contingency basis, the same as employment agencies, getting paid for their services only if and when they fill a particular job. The following list, published through the courtesy of the American Management Association, contains names of both search and contingency placement firms. For your purpose it doesn't really matter, although true search firms do not solicit job applicants (when they have an assignment, they go after the people they want).

Executive Placement Firms

Ahrens, Davis & Associates
20 Tower Lane
Avon, CT 06001
   Branches:
   Dallas, TX
   Los Angeles, CA

Antell, Nagel, Moorhead Associates
230 Park Avenue
New York, NY 10017

William B. Arnold Associates
1776 South Jackson Street
Denver, CO 80210

Asquith & Jackson Associates
Box 326
Weston, MA 02193

Nathan Barry Associates
301 Union Wharf
Boston, MA 02109

Martin H. Bauman, Inc.
410 Park Avenue
New York, NY 10022

Berk Associates
400 Stillson Road
Fairfield, CT 06430

Boyden Associates
260 Madison Avenue
New York, NY 10016
   Branches:
   Major cities in US and
   worldwide

Breitmayer Associates
72 Park Street
New Canaan, CT 06840
    Branch:
    New York, NY

Currie L. Brewer
750 Welch Road
Palo Alto, CA 94304

Brooks/Gay & Associates
50 Park Avenue
New York, NY 10016

D.A.K. Brown & Associates
342 Madison Avenue
New York, NY 10017
    Branch:
    Southport, CT

Burke & O'Brien Associates
233 Broadway
New York, NY 10007

Robert J. Bushee & Associates
P.O. Box 515
Carnegie, PA 15106

Camden & Associates
502 West Ogden
Hinsdale, IL 60521

Wm. T. Campbell & Associates
916 Esperson Building
Houston, TX
    Branch:
    New York, NY

Career Dynamics
P.O. Box 224
Boston, MA 02176

Chernuchin Associates
400 Madison Avenue
New York, NY 10017

Wm. H. Clark & Associates
330 Madison Avenue
New York, NY 10017
    Branches:
    Chicago, IL
    Los Angeles, CA

Cole, Warren & Long
2 Penn Center Plaza
Philadelphia, PA 19102

Grant Cooper & Associates
2388 Schuetz Road
St. Louis, MO 63141
    Branches:
    Los Angeles, Long Beach, CA

Corry, Howe Associates
Time Life Building
New York, NY 10020

Corwen-Marchant Associates
527 Madison Avenue
New York, NY 10022
    Branch:
    Willow Grove, PA

Datalink Associates
830 Post Road East
Westport, CT 06880

Thorndike Deland Associates
1440 Broadway
New York, NY 10018

Drake-Beam & Associates
277 Park Avenue
New York, NY 10017
    Branches:
    Des Plains, IL
    Houston, TX
    Costa Mesa, CA
    San Francisco, CA
    Pittsburgh, PA
    Washington, DC

Eastman & Bodine
111 East Monroe Street
Chicago, IL 60603
    Branches:
    New York, NY
    Los Angeles, CA

Ecrivant Corp.
2049 Century Park, East
Los Angeles, CA 90067

Einstein Associates
380 Lexington Avenue
New York, NY 10017

Emmons-Labus Associates
4000 Town Center
Southfield, MI 48075

Ernst Van Praaq, Inc.
135 East 55th Street
New York, NY 10022

Executive Manning Corp.
3000 N.E. 30th Place
Ft. Lauderdale, FL 33306

Foote, Waldron
310 108th Avenue, N.E.
Bellevue, WA 98007

40 Plus Membership
15 Park Row
New York, NY 10038
    Branches:
    Chicago, IL
    Denver, CO
    Houston, TX
    Los Angeles, Oakland, CA
    Philadelphia, PA
    Washington, DC

George W. Fotis & Associates
170 Mason Street
Greenwich, CT 06830

Fox-Morris Associates
1500 Chestnut Street
Philadelphia, PA 19102
    Branches:
    Atlanta, GA
    Baltimore, MD
    Charlotte, WV
    Cleveland, OH
    Houston, TX
    Los Angeles, CA
    New York, NY
    Pittsburgh, PA
    Princeton, NJ
    San Francisco, CA
    Wilmington, VA

Franklin Career Search
380 Madison Avenue
New York, NY 10016

Fredericks & Marshall
15910 Ventura Boulevard
Encino, CA 91436

J.B. Gilbert Associates
420 Lexington Avenue
New York, NY 10017

Goggi Associates
505 Thonrall Street
Edison, NJ 08817

Goodrich & Sherwood Co.
521 Fifth Avenue
New York, NY 10017

David Gootnick Associates
55 West 42nd Street
New York, NY 10036

J.B. Gorham & Co.
60 East 42nd Street
New York, NY 10017

Maxwell Gould Associates
31 Woodland Street
Hartford, CT 06105

Graham & Company
220 East 42nd Street
New York, NY 10017

Halbrecht Associates
695 Summer Street
Stamford, CT 06901
    Branches:
    New York, NY
    Washington, DC
    Chicago, IL

Handy Associates
245 Park Avenue
New York, NY 10017

Hawthorne, International
760 Summer Street
Stamford, CT 06904

Hazel Associates
60 East 42nd Street
New York, NY 10017

Health Industry Consultants
333 West Hamden Avenue
Englewood, CO 80110

F.P. Healy & Co.
630 Third Avenue
New York, NY 10017

Heidrick & Struggles, Inc.
125 South Wacker Drive
Chicago, IL 60606
Branches:
Atlanta, GA
Boston, MA
Cleveland, OH
Dallas, Houston, TX
Los Angeles, CA
New York, NY
San Francisco, CA

Robert Heller Associates
25 Valley Drive
Greenwich, CT 06830
Branches:
New York, NY
Washington, DC

Industry Search, Inc.
3100 Monroe Avenue
Rochester, NY 14618

Jaimlee Associates
717 Fifth Avenue
New York, NY 10022

Janus Consultants, Inc.
1212 Potomac Street
Washington, DC 20007

Judd-Falk, Inc.
124 East 37th Street
New York, NY 10016

Kahlert Associates
375 Park Avenue
New York, NY 10022
Branches:
Chicago, IL
Los Angeles, CA
San Francisco, CA
Houston, TX
Palm Beach, FL
New York, NY

A.T. Kearney, Inc.
100 South Wacker Drive
Chicago, IL 60606
Branches:
Cleveland, OH
Los Angeles, CA
New York, NY

Kenmore Personnel
555 Fifth Avenue
New York, NY 10017

Korn/Ferry International
277 Park Avenue
New York, NY 10017
Branches:
Los Angeles, CA
Chicago, IL
Houston, Dallas, TX
Atlanta, GA
San Francisco, CA
Cleveland, OH

Kunzer Associates
208 South LaSalle Street
Chicago, IL 60604

Lamson/Griffiths Associates
20 North Wacker Drive
Chicago, IL 60606

Robert E. Larson Associates
2300 North Mayfair Road
Milwaukee, WI

Lauer, Sbarbaro Associates
135 South LaSalle Street
Chicago, IL 60603

Arthur J. Lovely Associates
60 East 42nd Street
New York, NY 10017

Edward H. Lubin Associates
300 East 54th Street
New York, NY 10020

Ross MacAskill Associates
1660 L Street
Washington, DC 20036
Branches:
Denver, CO
Honolulu, HI
Newport Beach, CA
Portland, OR
Seattle, WA

Management Recruiters
1015 Euclid Street
Cleveland, OH 44115

Branches:
Most major cities

Man-Marketing Services
2610 Prudential Plaza
Chicago, IL 60601

William McCulloch Associates
20 East 46th Street
New York, NY 10017

McSherry & Associates
307 North Michigan Avenue
Chicago, IL 60601

Edward M. Melton Associates
15 Eton Road
Scarsdale, NY 10583

Menzel, Robinson, Baldwin
550 West Campus Drive
Arlington Heights, IL 60004

Robert Murphy Associates
230 Park Avenue
New York, NY 10017

Allen Oehmi Associates
470 Newark-Pompton Turnpike
Pompton Lakes, NJ 07444

Oliver & Rosner Associates
598 Madison Avenue
New York, NY 10022

PA Intl Management Consultants
200 Park Avenue
New York, NY 10017
    Branches:
    Chicago, IL, and other major
        cities

John Paisios & Associates
2222 Kensington Court
Oak Brook, IL 60521
    Branch:
    New Orleans, LA

Bruce Payne Consultants
1275 Time & Life Building
New York, NY 10020

Rene Plessner Associates
450 Park Avenue
New York, NY 10020

J. Redmond & Associates
57 North Street
Danbury, CT 06810
    Branch:
    White Plains, NY

Robert Reissig & Associates
4 Whitney Street Extension
Westport, CT 06880

Richard/Allen/Winter
222 Wisconsin Avenue
Lake Forest, IL 60045

Rolnick-Newman Associates
4615 Southwest Freeway
Houston, TX 77027

Allen Sarn Associates
527 Madison Avenue
New York, NY 10022

Schweigaard-Olsen
380 Madison Avenue
New York, NY 10017
    Branch:
    Washington, DC

Search Associates
12 Bank Street
Summit, NJ 07901

Search Consultants
10 Forest Avenue
Paramus, NJ 07652

William A. Sharon Associates
515 Madison Avenue
New York, NY 10022

Daniel A. Silverstein Associates
375 Park Avenue
New York, NY 10022

Specialized Search Associates
350 Madison Avenue
New York, NY 10017

Spencer, Stuart & Associates
437 Madison Avenue
New York, NY 10022
   Branches:
   Chicago, IL
   Dallas, TX
   Los Angeles, Stamford, Palo
     Alto, CA

William Stack Associates
230 Park Avenue
New York, NY 10017
   Branch:
   New Caanan, CT

L.W. Stern Associates
120 East 56th Street
New York, NY 10022

STM Executive Recruiters
350 South 400 East
Salt Lake City, UT 84111

The Charles Stuart Group
150 North Wacker Drive
Chicago, IL 60606

John S. Studwell Associates
310 Madison Avenue
New York, NY 10017
   Branches:
   Chicago, Hinsdale, IL
   San Francisco, CA
   Los Angeles, CA

Stumbaug Associates
4319 Covington Highway
Decatur, GA 30035

Victor Tabaka & Associates
430 King Road, N.W.
Atlanta, GA 30342

Harry F. Twomey Associates
1601 Walnut Street
Philadelphia, PA 19102

Waggett-Tawney Associates
1770 St. James Place
Houston, TX 77056

Wallinger Associates
12-16 Bank Street
Summit, NJ 07901
   Branches:
   All major cities

Webster Positions, Inc.
76 North Broadway
Hicksville, NY 11801

R.M. Whiteside Company
633 Third Avenue
New York, NY 10017

William H. Willis, Inc.
445 Park Avenue
New York, NY 10022

Wytmar & Co.
10 South Riverside Plaza
Chicago, IL 60603

Egon Zehnder, International
645 Fifth Avenue
New York, NY 10022

8

Job Services—
Approach With Care

There are job and career services that you may wish to consult. Unlike employment agencies and search firms, these do not find jobs. They offer advice, guidance, testing, resume writing and career planning, all of which are designed to make you a more effective job hunter. These services go by many names, but one thing that they all have in common is they all charge substantial fees.

High Fees with No Guarantees

Many of these firms are competent and staffed with professionals. There are also the opportunists who prey on the vulnerability of the unemployed. Unfortunately, there is no instant way to tell the difference.

Since they always charge fees and give no guarantees, be very careful if you decide to use their services. You will be spending time and money when you can least afford either.

Before using such a service, check the local Better Business Bureau. If their files show more than one complaint against the firm in the past year, look elsewhere. Call the local Consumer Protection Agency and check them too.

Read Before You Sign

If the firm you pick still looks good, make an appointment for a preliminary interview, and ask lots of questions. Request a copy of their contract to take home, or to show to a lawyer. If the firm refuses to let you have a copy of their contract to study before you sign, end the interview. You should be fully aware of the legal obligations you are undertaking when you sign any agreement.

Another important item: ask the firm for business references, specifically the names of some people it has served before. Then contact these people yourself.

One type of job consulting firm should be approached with special care: those offering overseas jobs. Their ads are enticing, but never actually promise a job overseas. They strongly imply that their contacts open doors to glamorous, high-paying jobs all over the world, but their actual service usually consists of mailing your resume to a list of firms with overseas branches.

If you are an engineer, computer technician, teacher, doctor or other highly specialized professional, and you want to work overseas, your chances of landing a job are good. If you have these credentials, you don't need a specialized job service. Any number of international firms or government agencies will accept your application.

9

The Public Employment Service

Job hunting, as you well know, can be a tedious and discouraging task. But the key to *successful* job hunting is thoroughness and attention to detail. That means following up leads and possibilities that are not very high on the scale of productivity, as well as those leads that can be expected to yield better results. In short, don't pass up any bets. After all, you haven't anything to lose.

One of the least productive areas for job hunting, but one that takes little time and effort, is the State Employment Service.

There is a State Employment Service in every state, with offices generally in every major city of that state. The State Employment Service has two principal functions. The first is to act as a registration center for those people collecting their unemployment benefits, and the second is to try and match applicants with available jobs.

The first function is pretty straightforward. In most cases, people collecting unemployment benefits *must* register with the State Employment Service, and have their books stamped periodically, or they run into trouble collecting benefits. This periodic registration proves that they are available for suitable jobs. In most cases, nothing tangible comes of this except that the applicant has fulfilled a detail of maintaining his or her eligibility for benefits.

The second function of the State Employment Service is to match jobs

42

with applicants. By and large, except in the case of lower salaried positions, the State Employment Service doesn't succeed. The reason is quite simple: most employers don't list jobs with the state agency (except in the case of industrial, domestic, restaurant and clerical jobs) because employers find they have to see too many unqualified people and have to make too many explanations to the agency when they don't hire someone.

Professional Placement Centers

In an attempt to upgrade their services, the State Employment agencies have, in many areas, established Professional Placement Centers, e.g., offices (some rather plush) where artists, accountants, nurses, corporate managers and indeed any professional applicant can be interviewed. Unfortunately, the record of these centers isn't very good on overall placements. The State Employment Service actually has a far better record with blue-collar placement than with white-collar.

Many state agencies are now tied into a Job Bank program, whereby listings from several states are fed into a computer and a printout is available to anyone who wants it. Thus an accountant can get an idea of what openings there are in Massachusetts as well as in California. While this is basically a good idea, it hasn't meant too much in actual placements.

The State Employment agencies are tied together in a network by the U.S. Employment Service, an agency of the U.S. Department of Labor. The USES is not a job placement agency. It serves as an advisor to state agencies, and funds a number of special programs that are administered through them. It also coordinates certain technical services to the state agencies.

The State Employment Service isn't one of the better bets. But it is worth a couple of hours to go through their routine (most of this time is spent waiting to see someone) and then making occasional checks with them to see if anything is there for you. And who knows—there might be. *Someone* has to win the lottery—you might as well have a shot at it too.

10

Women
in the Job Market

Looking for a job is never an easy task for anyone. If you are a woman, however, it is easier for you now than it has ever been.

That doesn't mean that all doors are automatically open for you—there is plenty of old-fashioned discrimination left. However, due to the activities of the various women's rights movements over the past decade, and resulting legislation, most corporations have gotten the message. Whether or not this is due to an attack of conscience is debatable. However the law now says the doors will be open or else, and companies are falling all over each other to comply.

If you have an MBA, the news is even better. Large firms are competing for the privilege of hiring women MBAs for their management training programs at substantial starting salaries, and they are not bashful in specifying that "men need not apply."

Women's Networks

Because of this new flurry of activity to hire women for jobs traditionally reserved for men, women have begun to share their job-hunting activities with each other in a system known as networking.

This is the female version of the old boy system which heretofore was the province of exclusive men's clubs, business associations and trade groups whose main purpose was to bring together individuals with common business interests. This technique of networking has been adopted by women's groups all over the country, and today there is scarcely a city that does not play host to workshops, symposiums and job clinics in almost every occupation. In addition, women have formed special groups to deal with such subjects as legal rights, self-awareness, professional career advancement and all kinds of similar activities whereby women can exchange information, learn job-hunting techniques and help themselves compete successfully in their chosen careers.

Following this chapter, on pages 54–55, there is a list of organizations that can provide information and assistance in this area.

Reentering the Job Market

If you are reentering the job market after a long absence, the task gets tougher.

Looking for a job in a highly competitive market is hard enough. Convincing a prospective employer that you can do the job after a long absence sometimes seems impossible.

One glance at the help wanted ads in the newspaper will probably throw you into a state of shock when you realize that you do not qualify for any of the jobs listed.

Plan Your Campaign

Having discovered that the business world is not eagerly awaiting your return, what do you do? First, suppress the panic. Then sit down with paper and pencil in hand and proceed to work out a plan.

Start off by writing an autobiography, starting somewhere around the time you graduated high school or college. Recall the subjects you liked or were good at in school, the jobs you held right up to the time you left the business world, the activities you liked and those at which you were best.

On another sheet of paper, list all of the skills you have. Try to identify your achievements and skills which are transferable no matter how minor or ordinary. Take into consideration your intangible assets, such as your ability to work with people, your tactfulness, your ability to persuade. Ask yourself questions: Do you work better with people or information? Are you creative? Are you basically a dynamic person or do you consider yourself low-key? Can you handle deadlines calmly or do you fall apart if you have to meet a tight schedule? Are you well-organized or do you do things haphazardly and without planning?

The information you include will help you write your resume. It will help you decide what kind of job you want.

Now list your job preferences. Then, taking each of your skills and aptitudes, try to match each one to the activities listed below:

selling	training
research	bookkeeping
writing	organization
statistics	public relations
administration	interviewing
advertising	marketing
accounting	market research

This will give you a general idea of where you can apply your natural aptitudes and learned skills and can provide you with some direction when answering ads and going after jobs.

If you are not sure of your aptitudes or what you want to do, avail yourself of the facilities of your State Employment Service. They provide free testing to anyone requesting it. You may have to press them for it, but it is available.

Be wary of private fee-charging counseling services. They can be expensive, and have not been known to provide many benefits to people whose current experience is limited.

Beware of Traps

There are certain pitfalls that the female job-seeker should look out for. First, you will notice that many help wanted ads are titled "Administrative Assistant." Actually, most of these firms are looking for secretaries. The term administrative assistant has become popular in the last ten years for two reasons: secretaries are in short supply, and most women do not want to be secretaries. Employers, desperate for secretarial help, try to disguise the nature of the job by giving it a more prestigious title.

Second, you will also notice that most of these ads call for good skills. This means shorthand and typing. If you have the skills and want to be a secretary, fine. Otherwise, forget it.

Another type of help wanted approach is pure baloney, and you will find this type used mostly in advertisements by employment agencies. These are for the so-called glamour jobs. While some of them actually exist, be very wary about taking them at face value. The title will be "administrative assistant," followed by large, bold type announcing, **GET INVOLVED—EXECUTIVE SUITE—TRAVEL FREE—AIRLINES —ART MUSEUM—WORK WITH PEOPLE—PUBLISHING.** Buried in the small copy will again be the words "good skills." The secret is there—another secretarial job.

Many employment agencies will try to sell you on a clerical position no matter what your qualifications. The key question is: "Can you type?" While this can be legitimate in certain jobs, such as editorial or public relations, be firm. If you are answering a specific ad for another type of job and you feel the agency is trying to talk you out of it, remind them of the laws against sex discrimination. They become very attentive when you cite statutes.

If you are trying to avoid a clerical job at all costs, stay away from the commercial agencies. Study the ads that agencies run and register only those that list professional jobs.

Employer Attitudes

Many employers will not consider women or men who have long gaps between jobs. They are especially suspicious of women looking for jobs after a long absence. Lack of skills and experience is only a part of their objections. They fear that if they hire such a woman, she may be retrained at company expense and then decide that the nine to five work day is not for her.

Others suspect that an older woman may wilt under the pressure of modern business or become bored with the routine. Fortunately, not all employers feel this way. Many, through bitter experience with young employees, have come to realize that mature women are more dependable, less demanding and less likely to switch jobs frequently.

Government Jobs

Investigate the job opportunities with the federal, state and local governments. Depending on your background and skills, there may be positions available.

If you live near a facility of the Internal Revenue Service, investigate the possibility of temporary or seasonal jobs. The IRS hires women in local areas during the periods of peak tax activity. If you get on the rolls as a seasonal employee, you can also collect unemployment insurance during lay-off periods.

Many government agencies make use of flex time. This means that you can work whatever hours you wish, giving you an opportunity to hold a job and devote time to your home and/or children.

Preparing the Resume

Reentering the job market after many years makes the job of preparing a resume more difficult. You cannot just list your experience (as is done on a chronological resume) if your last job ended eight years ago. Readers will think they lost a page somewhere. Therefore, your resume should be basically functional, with the emphasis on your skills, aptitudes and accomplishments. It should lead off with a detailed summary of your experience. Next, list the firms you worked for, with a description of your duties and responsibilities. Although most resumes list dates of employment, if you have been out of the job market for a number of years it is better to leave out dates. If interested in your background, the reader will ask for the dates.

Get the Interview

Your main objective when reentering the job market is to get a face-to-face interview, where you can sell your abilities personally. Avoid anything in a letter or resume that will discourage that chance. A sample of a resume for reentering the job market will be found on page 52.

It can sometimes be more advantageous to avoid the resume altogether and construct a letter in narrative form which describes your experience, qualifications and skills. Have the resume ready, however, for the interview, where you can explain your record in person. A copy of this type of letter will be found on page 51.

Be Selective

Women who reenter the job market may find a strong temptation to settle for the first thing that comes along. This may be due to lack of confidence, self-depreciation, or plain gratitude at finding someone who wants you. Give yourself an opportunity to investigate the job market thoroughly. If you take a job you really don't want because you're afraid you'll not be offered another, you will find yourself locked in with little opportunity and no freedom to see if there is anything better. Since you have already been out of the market for a long time, another month or two is not going to make that much difference.

Your Legal Rights

According to a survey taken by the Women's Bureau of the U.S. Department of Labor, women held more than two out of five jobs in the civilian labor force, but the average pay of those who work full-time the year round is only about three-fifths of the average for full-time year-round male workers. The situation is improving but there is still a wide gap.

Much of the pay differential is a result of the fact that women have traditionally had access only to low-paying jobs, have often been paid less than men for the same work, and have had limited opportunities. However, now written into law, and affirmed by numerous court cases, is the provision that in the labor market men and women must stand equal in opportunity for hiring and for pay when work is equal.

Problems in getting a job or in coping with the job situation often can be resolved through discussion with personnel officers or supervisors. In many firms, grievance procedures are available under equal opportunity programs.

However, if you believe that you are being paid less than a legal wage or that you are the victim of discrimination (prohibited by law), you are entitled to file a complaint with the appropriate agency. Procedures for making complaints vary—a telephone request is enough to set an investigation in motion, whereas a formal verified complaint is necessary under some antidiscrimination laws.

You have a right to complain if:

—an employment agency refuses to refer you to job openings;
—you are passed over for a promotion for which you are qualified;
—you are paid less than others for comparable work;
—you are left out of training or apprenticeship programs;

and the reason for any of these acts is your sex, race, color, religion or national origin.

Protection Against Age Discrimination

The Age Discrimination in Employment Act prohibits discrimination on the basis of age against any person between the ages of forty and seventy in hiring, firing, compensation or other conditions of employment. The law applies to all employers of 20 or more employees and employment agencies serving covered employers. It does not cover situations in which age is a bona fide occupational qualification (such as modeling junior miss fashions). It also prohibits using employee benefit plans as a basis for refusing to hire older applicants.

Tax Credit for Child Care and Household Help

Since 1954 a deduction (subtracted from gross income before computation of income tax) has been authorized for child and dependent care. You may take a credit of up to 20 percent of actual expenses for dependent care, provided the expenses are incurred to enable you to be gainfully employed, with a maximum amount payable for such expenses of $2,000 for the care of one dependent and $4,000 for the care of two or more dependents.

Information Sources

You will find on page 54 a list of magazines published for women in the workplace, plus a bibliography of books written for women on many aspects of job and careers. These are generally available at your library.

Re-entering the Job Market

SALLY DICKERSON   614-555-2465
411 North 12th St.
Cleveland, Ohio 44136

December 16, 1980

Standard Products Company
1410 Berwick Street
Cleveland, Ohio 44178

I am replying to your advertisement in the Cleveland Plain Dealer for a public relations assistant.

As a former member of a local health center that provides educational and informational services to 12,000 community residents, I have participated in planning and implementing fund raising events, public affairs, and media coverage.

This experience has given me an extremely good background in public affairs, including writing, editing, and researching. I have excellent administrative skills, having previously held a responsible office position with a real estate firm.

I would appreciate the privilege of an interview, where I can have the opportunity of presenting my qualifications to you in person.

Thank you for your consideration.

Sincerely,

SALLY DICKERSON

RESUME

SALLY DICKERSON
411 North 12th St.
Cleveland, Ohio 44136

(614) 555-2465

SUMMARY OF
EXPERIENCE

* Customer relations
* Supervision of office personnel
* Developed system for efficient use of forms
  to control work flow
* Wrote correspondence
* Researched information for clients
* Kept accounts payable and accounts receivable
  records
* Prepared public relations materials for fund
  raising
* Worked with radio and TV stations for support
  of medical facility
* Assisted president of firm in all aspects
  of administration

EMPLOYMENT

Roslyn Berks Health Center
1426 Euclid Avenue
Cleveland, Ohio

   Volunteer public affairs assistant for local
   treatment facility which performed services for
   12,000 people.

   My responsibilities included providing information to
   residents and patients on the functions and activities
   of the center -- planning fund raising events with
   local radio and television stations to promote the
   center as a public service -- worked with county
   officials in developing on-going programs.

M.R.Flanders Company, Inc.
4967 Avenue A
Pittsburgh, Pa.

   Assistant to the president of a small real estate
   office. In this position, I was responsible for the
   day-to-day operation of the office. This included
   posting all checks and invoices to proper ledger,
   supervising the typing of leases, answering inquiries
   and complaints from customers and tenants, showing

Sally Dickerson

properties to prospective buyers, maintaining liason
with city building officials, construction companies
and suppliers.

EDUCATION

University of Pittsburgh - 3 years
Majored in English

Western Pennsylvania Business School - 1 year
Accounting and business procedures

PERSONAL

Age 37
Married
Available immediately

Professional Women's Organizations

(Most of these organizations will send literature upon request. Some
provide job placement services.)

Advertising Women of New York, Inc.
153 East 57th Street
New York, NY 10022

American Business Women's Association
9100 Ward Parkway
Kansas City, MO 64114

American Medical Women's Association, Inc.
465 Grand Street
New York, NY 10002

American Society of Professional and Executive Women
1511 Walnut Street
Philadelphia, PA 19102

American Society of Women Accountants
Suite 1036, East Wacker Drive
Chicago, IL 60601

American Women in Radio and Television, Inc.
1321 Connecticut Avenue, N.W.
Washington, DC 20036

Association for Women in Science
1346 Connecticut Avenue, N.W.
Washington, DC 20036

Association of Women in Architecture
7440 University Drive
St. Louis, MO 63130

Business and Professional Women's Foundation
2012 Massachusetts Avenue, N.W.
Washington, DC 20036

Catalyst
14 East 60th Street
New York, NY 10022

Committee for Women in Public Administration
American Society for Public Administration
1255 Connecticut Avenue, N.W., Suite 300
Washington, DC 20036

Division for Women in Medicine
The Medical College of Pennsylvania
3300 Henry Avenue
Philadelphia, PA 19129

Federally Employed Women (FEW)
National Press Building, Suite 481
Washington, DC 20045

Financial Women's Association of New York
443 West 50th Street
New York, NY 10020

General Federation of Women's Clubs
1734 N Street, N.W.
Washington, DC 20036

National Association of Bank Women, Inc.
111 East Wacker Drive
Chicago, IL 60601

National Association of Bank Women
Union Bank Building
4201 Long Beach Boulevard
Long Beach, CA 90807

National Association of Bank Women, Inc.
35 East 72nd Street
New York, NY 10021

National Association of Female Executives
32 East 39th Street
New York, NY 10016

National Association of Insurance Women
1847 East 15th Street
Tulsa, OK 74104

National Association of Women Artists
41 Union Square
New York, NY 10003

National Federation of Business and Professional Women's Clubs, Inc.
2012 Massachusetts Avenue, N.W.
Washington, DC 20011

National Organization for Women
425 13th Street, Suite 1001
Washington, DC 20004

Society of Women Engineers
345 East 47th Street
New York, NY 10017

Women in Communications, Inc.
P.O. Box 9561
Austin, TX 78766

Magazines for Working Women

ESSENCE
1500 Broadway
New York, NY 10036

For young black women.

GRADUATE WOMAN
American Association of University
    Women
2401 Virginia Avenue, N.W.
Washington, DC 20037

Edited for action-oriented women
concerned with women's
issues, problems, history—
primarily by, for and about
women.

MS.
MS. Foundation for Education &
    Communication, Inc.
370 Lexington Avenue
New York, NY 10017

Forum for women and men to
share information about
their changing roles.

NEW WOMAN
New Woman, Inc.
P.O. Drawer 189
Palm Beach, FL 33480

Guidance, information, and way-
of-life for active women in
all walks of life, careers; new
styles in marriage.

SAVVY
111 Eighth Avenue
New York, NY 10011

For success-oriented career women.

SELF
Conde-Nast Publications
350 Madison Avenue
New York, NY 10017

Edited for women who enjoy their
careers as the focal point of
their lives.

WORKING MOTHER
McCall Publishing Co.
230 Park Avenue
New York, NY 10017

For working women with children
under 18 years living in the
household.

WORKING WOMAN
600 Madison Avenue
New York, NY 10022

For the career woman, with articles
on finance, jobs, business.

(Reader descriptions provided by publishers.)

Books for Working Women

Adams, Carolyn and Winston, Kathryn, *Mothers At Work*, New York: Longman.

Agassi, Judith B., *Women on the Job*, Lexington, Mass.: Lexington Books.

Bird, Caroline, *Everything A Woman Needs to Know to Get Paid What She's Worth*, New York: McKay.

Blair, Francine, *Equal Pay in the Office*, Lexington, Mass.: Lexington Books.

Boothe, Anna, *Job Hunting That Works*, Creative Arts Books.

Cohen, William A., *The Creative Guide to Finding A Superior Job*, New York, N.Y.: Amacom.

Eolis, Wendeen, *How To Write Effective Resumes*, New York, N.Y.: Barron.

Harrigan, Betty, *Games Mother Never Taught You: Corporate Gamemanship For Women*.

Hart, Lois Borland, *Moving Up—Women and Leadership*, New York, N.Y.: Amacom.

Henning, Margaret and Jardim, Anne, *The Managerial Woman*, Garden City, N.Y.: Doubleday & Company.

Higginson, Margaret V., and Quick, Thomas, L., *Ambitious Woman's Guide to a Successful Career, The*, New York, N.Y.: Amacom.

Jewell, Donald O., *Women And Management: An Expanding Role*, Atlanta, Ga.: Georgia State University Press.

Kennedy, James, H., *Women in Executive Recruiting*, Fitzwilliam, N.H.: Consultants News.

Kleiman, Carol, *Women's Networks: The Complete Guide to Getting A Better Job, Advancing Your Career and Feeling Great As A Woman Through Networking*, New York, N.Y.: Lippincott and Crowell.

Lembeck, Ruth, *Job Ideas for Today's Woman*, Englewood Cliffs, N.J.: Prentice-Hall, Inc.

Loring, Rosalind K. and Otto, Herbert A., *New Life Options: The Working Women's Resource Book*, New York, N.Y.: McGraw-Hill Book Co.

Myers, Henry, *Women At Work*, Princeton, N.J.: Dow Jones Books.

Pell, Arthur R., *Women's Guide to Management Positions*, New York, N.Y.: Monarch Press.

Schwartz, Felice, *How to go to Work When Your Husband is Against it, Your Children Aren't Old Enough, and There's Nothing you Can do Anyhow*, New York, N.Y.: Simon & Shuster.

11

Starting Out— Your First Job

Entering the job market for the first time is somewhat like going out on your first date. It can be frightening, educational, frustrating and embarrassing.

If you know what to expect, are aware of the pitfalls and use your initiative, entering the job market can also be rewarding and satisfying. The ease or difficulty with which you find your first job can depend on many things over which you have little or no control, such as the state of the economy, the demand for your occupational specialty, the size and economic health of your community, your education and training and your financial circumstances. All of these affect your chances of finding the job you want.

More important, however, are the factors over which you do have control—adequate preparation, knowledge of the market, an effective resume, a good interviewing technique, imagination, a determination to succeed and the stamina to do lots of plugging and hard work.

 ## Where to Look

If you are graduating soon or have just graduated, a good place to start is your school's placement department. High school placement offices usually have listings of local companies. College placement offices have national listings.

Most large corporations send recruiters to campuses all over the country to find new talent for their training programs. If you didn't avail yourself of this service while in school, you can still contact your placement officer for information on companies who recruited on campus, get the name of the recruiter and contact him or her by mail.

If you have decided what you would like to do and what kind of firm you would like to work for, you can aim your job-hunting campaign at specific targets. Consult a copy of *Standard & Poor's Directory of Corporations*. You can find it at most main public libraries. Firms are listed geographically. The information listed for each corporation includes the number of employees, location of plants and offices, names of executives with titles, products or services and dollar sales volume.

If you want additional and more current information about a company, call any stock brokerage firm in your area or contact the firm and ask that they send you a copy of the current annual report. Of course, these are only available from publicly-held corporations, but when available, they provide very complete and detailed information.

When you have chosen the companies that you would like to work for, proceed with the instructions given in the chapter on direct mail, which will tell you how to approach them for the best results.

Help Wanted Advertising

While you are contacting these firms through direct mail, don't ignore the classified ads in your local newspaper. These jobs are available *now*. Your letters to companies are speculative.

When using classified advertising, do not make the mistake of many neophytes in their first job hunt—answering ads that are obviously directed to applicants with years of experience. If a company is advertising a job that pays $25,000 a year, don't waste your time and the company's time by answering it. No matter how great you think you are, no one is going to pay a trainee $25,000 (unless you are a Harvard Business School graduate). Use your time wisely by responding to ads that have some relationship to your employment record or career goal.

Recent graduates frequently apply for positions paying $35,000 a year. When told that they need at least ten years of experience, some indignantly respond that if the job required experience, it should have been stated in the ad. The fact that there is a relationship between salaries and experience never occurs to a lot of beginners.

Although you should read all the help wanted ads in your newspapers, pay particular attention to those headed **College Grads—Management Trainees**—Trainees, and any position with the word Jr. attached to it.

Employment agencies are a good source for those just starting out. Many companies list entry-level jobs with agencies to avoid having to screen the large numbers of applications they would get if they advertised the position directly.

Making Up Your Mind

The two main problems you face are the relatively small number of entry-level positions open, and the large number of people competing for these jobs. The age-old question of how to get a job without experience, and how to get experience without a job, is still largely unanswered. But don't get discouraged. Millions of new workers enter the job force each year and the system creaks along pretty well. Of course, it's obvious that not everyone ends up in the kind of job that she or he really wants, and there are still too many who remain unemployed for long periods of time. But with the right attitude, perseverance and a willingness to listen to advice, you can run ahead of the statistics.

As a beginner facing the prospect of your first job, you may think you are about to make the most important decision of your life. You're not. There is generally more indecisiveness among young people looking for their first jobs than there is among more experienced job-seekers. In reality, your first job is your least important one.

Faced with a job offer, the young applicant fresh out of school tends to overanalyze all aspects of the position, including starting salary, benefits, future potential, the size of the firm, its political, social and economic posture. This only results in immobilizing the applicant's decision-making ability. Applicants who are fearful of accepting a position that might not be exactly the right one wind up looking far beyond a reasonable length of time—and lose income and valuable experience in the interim.

Most people will probably have more than one job in their lifetime, and some will have many. Each subsequent change becomes more important to your career and to your future. In your first position there are only two factors to consider: (1) that it is in, or related to, the field that you have chosen, and (2) that the company has some substance to it (you can learn more by working for a smaller firm, but generally avoid companies with very few employees).

Don't worry about advancement at this stage, and do not become overly concerned with money. Starting salaries are generally low. Unless your economic situation dictates a certain minimum, consider salary secondary. You are looking for an opportunity; if you are successful, the money will follow. Many beginning applicants lose excellent opportunities because they set a minimum salary for themselves at the wrong time.

The objective is to get started, to see what it's like to hold your first position, to learn something about the business world in general and your field in particular—and to earn an income. Remember, it's only your first job. Use it to get experience. If you're lucky, it could turn out to be the firm in which you make your career. It doesn't happen very often, but it's possible. More likely, it will be your first step up the ladder. You do not make a lifetime contract with your new employer. When you think you have learned enough, go on to the next job.

Your Image

A word about dress and appearance. Whatever your opinions are about hair length and clothing style, accept the fact that companies are not enchanted with unkempt beards, Mongolian mustaches and Harpo Marx hairdos, nor do they feel obliged to accept items such as shimmering eye shadow, four-inch eyelashes, two-tone hair or stick-on beauty marks—on either men or women.

For men: wear suits (matching jackets and trousers). No sport jacket and slacks at the interview. If you don't own a suit, buy one. You can always use it for weddings and funerals.

For women: wear a dress, or a skirt and blouse. No mu-mus, or illustrated t-shirts.

As for the people's uniform, denim jeans, save them for leisure activities. While it is true that modern dress is much more informal than it used to be, your image is all you have to sell at the outset, and it should be traditional and conservative. Once you have the job, you can adjust to the customs of the firm in which you are employed.

Winning Ways

Your resume is part of your overall presentation. It should be well-written, clean and contain all the pertinent facts about you and your background. Refer to the appropriate samples of resumes, cover letters and letters of application. These examples are designed for the young applicant seeking his or her first job. Use them as a guide. They have worked for others, and they can work for you.

One of the best ways to make a good impression on an interview is to show your interviewer that you have done your homework and know something about the company. While every job applicant should make a study of the firm she or he is interviewing with, it is particularly important for the first-job applicant who has no experience and whose background and education differs very little from other first-job applicants. Before you go into an interview, learn as much as you can about the company—its size, its products, services, sales volume, branch offices and plants. This information can be obtained at your local library and from the directories and reference books listed on pages 177–178.

The first thing you should do after your interview is to sit down and compose a bread-and-butter note. In it thank your interviewer for the opportunity of meeting him or her, and express the hope that you are being considered for the job. Even if you are not interested in working for the company at this point, it is better to leave all doors open until you have to make a final decision. The thank you note works wonders and will put you ahead of your competition. Samples of these letters will be found on pages 128 to 133.

12

Resumes—Their Use and Misuse

The most common word in the business of job-hunting is resume. The personnel world floats on a sea of resumes. The United States Post Office moves tons of resumes each day and employment agencies and companies are deluged by a blizzard of resumes.

Applicants hate them.

Personnel managers and assistants love them. No matter what you think of them, you must have one to get a job. If this is your first trip into the job market, you will soon discover what the veterans know—the whole world is resume-happy.

Walk into an employment agency or a corporate personnel office without a resume and you will find the atmosphere extremely chilly. Personnel people are programmed to ask for a resume before the applicant's coat is off. Employment agencies will request resumes of anyone who walks into the office (including the telephone installer).

According to the National Association of Personnel Consultants, 95 percent of all white-collar jobs are screened by the use of resumes. Worse than not having a resume is telling someone you don't believe in them. It's almost as unpatriotic as saying you don't believe in television or General Motors.

Why this almost irrational concern for resumes? Some reasons are logical, some are not—and some are downright illegal.

Resumes:

(1) can disclose age. Yes, Virginia, there *is* age discrimination. There is a law against it, but it doesn't take much ingenuity to get around the matter. And don't think that because you leave your age off the resume you are fooling someone. It doesn't require a PhD in mathematics to determine your age from a resume by adding up the years that have elapsed since you completed college or served in the armed forces. As a matter of fact, the one sure way to invite suspicion that you are tottering on the brink of senility is the absence of age or date of birth on your resume. The typical reaction to such a resume is an analysis of your background, your education and your work experience. A personnel clerk doesn't have to be Sherlock Holmes to get within a year or two of your age. Simple arithmetic does the trick.

(2) give the interviewer a lead in preparing questions for the interview. She knows a lot about you before you step into her office, while you have to play it by ear. She can decide in advance what questions to ask you about specific items on your resume, and have an entire game plan set up before you even know her name.

(3) can be read and evaluated by more than one person in the company before you are called in. Most personnel people pass resumes on to department heads for evaluation.

(4) provide a crutch for incompetent and lazy personnel people. It makes their job easier (but not yours). What can resumes do for you, the applicant?

Resumes:

(1) can drive you crazy trying to tailor them to fit every job for which you apply.

(2) can turn you into a professional resume writer. (When unable to land a job, you are driven to rewrite your resume over and over again, in an attempt to find the perfect formula.)

(3) can sour you against the whole job-hunting system and make you more cynical than you already are.

(4) can, if not closely controlled in their distribution, create a danger for you if you are employed.

(5) force you to compete with other resume writers and not with other job applicants for a job. A better resume writer with inferior credentials may get the interview that should go to you.

So why resumes? Because companies demand them. It would require the reeducation of a generation of personnel managers to eliminate the urge for resumes and establish a system whereby employer can meet with applicant without them. In the meantime, it is advisable to play the game and conform. Your livelihood depends on it.

In this chapter, you will learn how to prepare a resume and how to use it effectively. Later, you will see how it is possible to avoid using a resume and still get an interview.

Neatness Counts

The general appearance of your resume is very important. A plethora of resumes descends upon personnel departments and employment offices every working day. Even when no active recruiting is taking place, personnel departments of well-known firms are deluged with resumes from people in every occupation, at every level of experience. If your resume is printed badly, soiled or otherwise unattractive, it will receive little or no attention.

Although resumes are supposed to be screened to determine qualifications, in practice an entirely different concept comes into play. They are, in fact, read with the purpose of finding disqualifying data. At best, these are quickly put aside, to be filed away in some file cabinet. At worst . . . they may be cut up for use as scrap paper.

Several personnel managers have told me that the first reading of a resume is simply a fast screening to determine which of three files to put it in. Whatever name they give these files, it comes down to *yes—maybe —no*. The first two will get a second, more thorough reading, but if your resume falls into the last category you don't get another chance. It's a little like Russian roulette. The quickest way into the *no* file is a sloppy, carelessly prepared resume, badly reproduced, containing spelling errors, erasures and strike-overs. Handwritten resumes (yes, they are still sent) are not even given the privilege of the *no* file; they are usually dropped into the round file under the desk. The reasoning behind this seemingly arbitrary selection process goes like this: the care that goes into the preparation of a resume reflects the individual who prepares it. It would be a shame to lose a chance for an interview because you did not take the time and effort to follow a few simple rules of resume writing.

Before we get into the actual writing of the resume let's look at its physical make-up. It should always be on $8\frac{1}{2}'' \times 11''$ paper, of good quality. How many pages should a resume be? If you cannot fit all you have to say on two pages, you are either saying it badly or saying too much. Remember, a resume is a brief introduction of your background, not an autobiography. If you feel you cannot possibly do justice to yourself in two pages, go back over every paragraph and cut.

There was once a school of thought that said that every resume you submitted had to be a typewritten original, in order to be personal. There was also a school of thought that said if you submitted a typewritten original, it looked as if you were making up a different resume for each job for which you applied (constructing a resume to fit every job). Don't worry about it. It makes no difference whether your resume is typed or reproduced, so long as it is neat and legible. If you are a speed typist and enjoy pounding the keys day and night, you can type each of your resumes individually, but there is no reason to do this. Companies know you are contacting other firms and they are willing to accept reproduced resumes.

Resume reproduction is a thriving specialty for small printing firms, and no matter where you live there are probably several. Your telephone directory is the best source. The service is usually fast and relatively inexpensive. If you want to save a few dollars and have a late model electric typewriter at your disposal, you can make your own master copy, which the printer can reproduce by photo offset. If you use this method, be sure your copy is sharp and clean. Any smudges or errors will appear on your final resume, as your copy is reproduced photographically. For a few dollars more, the printer will retype your resume on an electric machine. With this method you will be able to choose the type style you want and be assured of a perfectly reproduced resume to enhance your chance for an interview.

 ## What Should Go Into a Resume?

The variety of resumes that come into personnel departments are infinite. There are short ones and long ones, clean ones and dirty ones. They are typed, printed, mimeographed and Xeroxed. Some are very formal. Some are too cute. Some are illegible. Some arrive without names and addresses.

Successful resumes—those that get job interviews—fall into one of four basic categories:

chronological	combination
functional	entry level

Which type you use depends on several factors:

your objective	work record
experience	occupation

(At the end of this chapter are sample resumes for each type.)

All resumes, no matter which form you use, must include the following information:

vital statistics: name, address, phone number
title, objective or position desired
work experience
education
miscellaneous information

As we have said before, resumes do not get jobs. They are designed to get interviews. It is sad, but true, that many qualified, competent applicants never get invited to interviews, because their resumes do not clearly and adequately present their qualifications to the reader. What is the sense of being a genius if you cannot convince anyone else?

Following is a description of each type of resume and the circumstances in which to use—and to avoid it.

The Chronological Resume

The chronological resume is most commonly used and is best for those with at least two years of experience. It is, as the name implies, a history of your education and experience arranged in reverse order, with your last position listed first. As you will see in the sample, it affords the reader a quick look at what and where you are today and enables the reader to trace your career back to your first job. Of course, the resume includes much more than that, but the format of the chronological resume presents your background in an easy-to-read sequence.

Let us construct a chronological resume step-by-step.

First, your name, address and telephone number appear at the top of the page. If you think this is too obvious to mention, you may be surprised to learn that some resumes come into offices without any personal identification. The writers of such careless resumes probably never figure out why they receive no responses.

The next heading is optional. It can be a title, your objective or position desired—or a combination of all three. Refer to the sample resumes to see how they are used. If you use a title in the heading of your resume, be sure it fits in with your experience. The danger of using titles in a mass-produced resume is that your title may not always fit well into a corporate structure. You may have been a comptroller of a small or medium-sized firm, but if you use the title of comptroller you may be eliminating yourself from a position with a large company where the title of assistant comptroller may carry more responsibility than your present position.

More important, if you are using the direct mail method of reaching companies, the use of a specific management title may cause your resume to be directed into the nearest paper shredder by the person who already has that title.

Job Objective or Position Desired should be a short statement reflecting your immediate and near-future goals. Avoid ending the long-range objective or position desired statement with comments like "leading to an executive position" or "to become a member of the management team." They are not only unnecessary but presumptuous. Inherent in the hiring of any individual for almost any position is the hope on both sides that it will lead to bigger and better things.

The major purpose of your resume is to obtain an interview leading to a currently available position. So keep the heading relevant and specific.

Work Experience

All resumes, regardless of their format, should include the following information about your experience:

> dates of employment
> name of previous firms and their complete addresses
> previous company's products or services
> your position
> brief description of your responsibilities
> specific accomplishments in your job

Dates of Employment—List your last or present employer first. This is vital. Employers are more interested in your most recent experience, and they are accustomed to reading resumes with the work experience listed from the last to the first job.

In the chronological resume, start with the inclusive date of employment (present job)—month and year started are sufficient. Follow with the full name of the firm and its complete address. Follow that with a list of the firm's products or services.

Next, list the title of each position you held, followed by a brief description of your duties, responsibilities and accomplishments. It is in this paragraph that you use a bit of salesmanship to convince a prospective employer that you can do a good job for him, just as you did for your other employers.

Do not get too wordy in listing your duties. It is not necessary to describe a typical day at the office—just the highlights will do. Follow this paragraph with a short statement about your accomplishments, however modest.

Given the size and complexities of most corporations today, it is not always easy to point to a single employee's contribution. However, if you look closely enough, you can probably find some area in your activities that resulted in an increase in efficiency or production. The sample resumes show how to handle this part of your experience.

Your Education—The amount of emphasis you give your education on your resume depends upon three factors: how long you have been out of school, what you studied and how much work experience you have.

The further away you are from graduation, the less important it is on your resume. Obviously, those seeking entry level jobs or who have light work experience must give more weight to their education. If you are in this category you should elaborate on your courses, even listing subjects —but only so long as they relate specifically to your career goals. Use discretion in deciding what to list and what to omit.

If you majored in Hindu philosophy, social progress under Louis IV or classical Sanskrit, and you are seeking a job in advertising, state that you have a BA or BS degree. You may have enjoyed the education and be a more informed person because of it, but esoteric subjects do not impress business executives, who are more interested in your ability to analyze a profit and loss statement.

However, if your education has specific application to the occupation or position you seek, exploit it for all it is worth. Study the sample resumes to see how education is described according to individual backgrounds.

Miscellaneous Information—Under *Miscellaneous* or *Personal*, list any data that you deem necessary for a prospective employer. Membership in professional and business organizations will show that you are interested enough in your career to give personal, unpaid time to extracurricular activities in your field. Do not, however, list social clubs or religious affiliations. They are not germane to your resume and are nobody's business. *Marital status*: you may list it if you wish. Laws in some states prohibit discrimination due to marital status. However, most employers feel that they are entitled to know whether you are married or single. The payroll department has to know for tax deductions anyway, so you might as well put it on your resume. *Your race and religion*: absolutely *not*. It has nothing to do with your job qualifications and has no place in the resume.

References: premature at this time. When there is enough interest in you as a prospect, the subject will come up. You can simply write, "Available on request."

Although the chronological form will adequately serve the majority of job candidates, there are circumstances where this type of resume can be harmful. They are:

(1) your work background is spotty and you have long periods of unaccounted time between jobs.

(2) you have a great deal of experience and are on the job market at a time when other people your age are looking forward to retirement.

(3) you want to change careers and switch to an entirely different occupation.

(4) you are a raw beginner with no experience at all.

Chronological Resume

LAWRENCE PRAEGER
131 Flatlands Avenue
Houston, Texas   77035   (713) 599-6645

OBJECTIVE

To obtain a position with a dynamic
company where my experience in office
management and administration will
contribute to its growth and profit.

EXPERIENCE

ARISTA PRINTING COMPANY, INC.
926 Mallow Avenue
Houston, Texas

Office Manager   April 1973 – Present

In charge of the main office of a printing firm grossing
in excess of one million dollars annually.

As office manager, I have complete responsibility for an office
employing 27 clerical and administrative people.

My responsibilities include: customer service, correspondence,
accounts receivable, accounts payable, payroll, bookkeeping,
cash disbursements, promotional mailings, purchasing office
supplies and instituting new systems for improving office
organization and work flow.

My position also entails the scheduling of work, follow-up
on completion, liason between office, plant and customers,
personnel evaluation, hiring and replacement, and miscellaneous
administrative duties. I report directly to the president of
the firm.

GARBER PEN COMPANY, INC.
725 Flushing Blvd.
Houston, Texas

Office Assistant   June 1971 – March 1973

Performed general clerical duties for a large manufactuter of
writing instruments. My work included bookkeeping, filing,
preparing freight and shipping documents and maintaining
inventory control records.

EDUCATION

University of Texas, Austin, Texas   1969 – 1970

Southeastern School of Business, Houston, Texas 1970 – 1971

PERSONAL

Born: December 4, 1953   Single   Excellent health

71

Chronological Resume

R E S U M E

Telephone: (302) 332-6954

Winston A. Davidson
1211 Hazleton Street
Wilmington, Del. 19805

PUBLIC RELATIONS MANAGER

SUMMARY:
Fifteen years experience in development, planning and implementation of corporate public relations programs. Background includes press relations, news and feature writing, employee communications, media placement, product publicity, speech writing and administration.

EXPERIENCE:
January 1979 to present

Director of Public Affairs

Delaware National Bank & Trust Company
Wilmington, Delaware

Among my major assignments were:
(1) Organizing and executing a public affairs program for this major financial organization, designed to acquaint the public with our involvement in community affairs such as education, health, and environmental problems.

(2) Responsibility for publication of booklets and pamphlets for internal distribution, dealing with the company's employment practices.

(3) Creation of a series of booklets, for distribution to customers and stockholders, on financial plans and policies.

December 1970 to December 1978

Director of Communications

Industrial Dynamics Corporation
Dover, Delaware

Responsible for complete public relations program including:

(1) Writing product publicity for the trade press.

(2) Contact and liaison with newspaper and magazine business editors for the purpose of placement of articles and stories relative to the company's product and services.

(3) Overseeing the writing and production
     of the company house organ.

(4) Writing speeches for the President and
     other senior officers of the firm for
     delivery to business and government interests.

February 1967 to March 1969

Assistant to Director of Press Relations

International Supermarkets, Inc.
Los Angeles, California

Assisted in planning and executing varied programs
of corporate public relations for major food
chain.

Responsibilities included speech writing,
preparation of annual reports, news and feature
stories on special promotions.

Maintained daily press relations with local
media.

1963 to 1968

Public Information Officer

U.S. Army
Fort Dix, New Jersey

EDUCATION: B.A., Journalism
              University of Delaware
              Newark, Delaware

              Graduate studies
              Pennsylvania State University
              State College, Pa.

PERSONAL: Member of the Publicity Club of Delaware
              Member of the American Association of Business
              Communicators

              Age: 38
              Married - 2 children
              Available for relocation

Chronological Resume

RESUME

IRVING BROITMAN
18 S. Van Buren St.
Boston, Mass. 02053

(617) 721-8645

Job Objective

A responsible position in Systems or Administration which will utilize my experience and provide an opportunity for personal advancement while making a real contribution to the growth of the organization.

Business Experience

1974
Present

National General Insurance Company, 1826 High Street, Boston, Mass.

Systems Manager

Supervise a group of 19 systems analysts engaged in

- Administrative systems
- Work measurement studies
- Equipment evaluation
- EDP applications
- Cost control programs
- Procedures development

1968
1974

Radcliffe & Company, 412 Main St., Boston, Mass.

Manual Systems Analyst

Conducted basic systems surveys, performed feasibility studies, and cost-benefits analyses in: accounts receivable, credit, financial information, order entry and distribution, to improve on present manual systems and provide a firm foundation for future automated systems.

- Reduced annual cost of operations by $240,000.
- Shortened payment and order processing time by 60%.
- Installed a work measurement and control program resulting in estimated annual savings of $800,000.

1962
1968

Bay Area Gas Company, Boston Mass.

Administrative Systems Analyst

- Developed and wrote operating procedures.
- Traveled to branch offices to analyze and

improve clerical systems.
- Prepared detailed operations reports for senior
management.

Education

Temple University, Philadelphia, Pa.
B.A. degree - economics
Graduated 1960

New York University Graduate School of Business
MBA - Business Management
Received 1962

Associations

American Management Association
New England Association of Systems Managers
Dale Carnegie Institute - Assistant instructor

Personal

Born: October 17, 1940
Married
Four children

Chronological Resume

R E S U M E

Howard H. Johnson   Home phone: 555-3745
1834 W. 34th St.   Office   :   666-4813
New York, N.Y. 10014

OBJECTIVE: To obtain an accounting position that would
              provide an opportunity for professional growth
              and development.

EDUCATION: New York University
              New York, N.Y.

              Bachelor of Science - Accounting - June 1971
                   Grades: Overall - 3.5
                           Major   - 4.0
                           Dean's List - 3 semesters

              Staten Island Community College
              Staten Island, New York

              Associate of Arts - Accounting - January 1969

EXPERIENCE:

February 1977 - Present
              Jeanne Ray Lowenstein, P.C.
              Certified Public Accountants
              318 Madison Avenue
              New York, N.Y. 10017

              Position: Staff Auditor -- Assignments entailed
                        the performance of certified audits
                        for diversified firms, such as retailing,
                        manufacturing, construction, shipping
                        and real estate.

                        Auditing duties include preparation
                        of corporate and partnership tax returns
                        plus payroll tax returns for clients.

                        I received special commendation from
                        the president of the firm for having
                        developed a client scheduling system
                        which resulted in better utilization of
                        time in servicing out-of-town accounts.

June 1973 - June 1977
              Rosser Business Forms, Inc.
              426 Main Street
              White Plains, N.Y. 11698

Howard H. Johnson (2)

Position: Accountant -- duties included journal
entry preparation, account analysis,
preparation of quarterly tax returns,
bank reconciliations and preparation
of financial statements.

Additional responsibilities consisted
of preparation of tax returns of
senior officers of the firm. Worked
closely with outside auditors.

June 1971 - January 1973
National Life Insurance Co.
1286 Seventh Ave.
New York, N.Y. 10022

Position: Acccounting Clerk -- Duties consisted
of preparation of actuarial tables and
checking the accuracy of mathematical
formulas used in computing premium
rate charts.

Performed other junior accounting
functions such as ledger entry, bank
deposits, preparation of monthly
premium reconciliation records.

MISCELLANEOUS:

Date of birth: February 26, 1950
Height: 6'1"
Weight: 176 lbs.
Single
Willing to travel and relocate

Chronological Resume

Gerald Kadich   126 Dayview Road
                                       Lambertville, N.J. 08661

(609) 555-8143 - Home
(609) 555-4800 - Office

EXPERIENCE SUMMARY

Financial Analyst

Financial analysis, budgeting, forecasting, profit planning,
capital expenditures and risk analysis, investment analysis
and planning, market research, business acquisition studies,
standard costing, financial/economic models, special projects.

EDUCATION

M.B.A., Finance, University of Pennsylvania, Philadelphia, Pa.
B.S., Economics, Wharton School of Finance, Philadelphia, Pa.

EMPLOYMENT HISTORY

March, 1975 - Present
Liberty Power Company, Trenton, N.J.

Major Responsbility: Planning and implementation of special
projects, new products, cost reductions, capital expenditures,
standard product costs, cost variance analysis.

Special Accomplishments: Developed and implemented manufacturing plans which included financial planning for two new products,
cost reduction and capital expenditures programs. Prepared
product performance reports and strategic plans adopted by
management for profit maximation.

June, 1973 - January, 1975
Pennsylvania Electronics Co., Inc., Philadelphia, Pa.

Major Responsibility: Product line value analysis, standard
costing, technical and financial analysis, planning for cost
reductions and capital expenditures.
Accomplishments: Developed and implemented action plan for
products cost reduction which resulted in over $200,000 annual
savings.

August, 1971 - June, 1973

Delaware Valley Industrial Corporation, Bala Cynwyd, Pa.
Major Responsibility: Accountant and junior financial analyst.

June, 1966 - July, 1971

Lenox Instrument Company, Trenton, N.J.
Major Responsibility: Junior Accountant.

PERSONAL

Born: April 3, 1943   Married/One child   Travel/Relocate

The Functional Resume

Unlike the chronological resume, which presents your background in an orderly year-by-year fashion from your last job to your first, the functional resume concentrates on what you have done rather than for whom and for how long. Its purpose is to draw attention away from facts which may be detrimental to you—not to hide them. This resume contains the same information as the chronological resume. It is just arranged differently.

After you have written the heading, your name, address, telephone number and objective (as in the chronological resume), you start off with as many short paragraphs as you need to describe the jobs you have had together with your duties and responsibilities. Written in narrative form, this description will be more detailed than it would be on a chronological resume. Since you have more freedom to elaborate, you can show such items as who you reported to, how many people you supervised, any special responsibilities you might have held. List all of the positions you held with the same company in a separate paragraph for each, so that the reader can get an idea of your exact progress through the firm.

Your next heading, education, should be in the same form as the chronological resume.

The next section should be a straightforward listing of the firms you worked for. Include the name and the address—nothing more. The emphasis in the functional resume is on what you have done, not how long ago it was done. By the time the reader has reached this portion of the resume, it is hoped that she or he will be sold on your qualifications and convinced that an interview would be productive.

This type of resume is especially recommended for those who might face an age barrier. By concentrating on your accomplishments with a functional resume, your chances of getting an interview are greater than if you listed twenty years of employment on a chronological resume.

The functional resume is also effective for those interested in changing careers. If you have been employed for a long period of time in one type of work or in one industry and want to switch to something entirely different, the chronological resume would only reinforce your past experience. By constructing a functional resume, you can thoroughly describe your abilities and your aptitudes. For instance, if you were a salesperson all of your life and were looking for another sales position, you would normally prepare a chronological resume that would show how you increased sales volume and developed new accounts for your past and present employers. If you wanted to get out of sales and thought that you might enjoy being in the personnel field, the chronological resume would most likely be ignored by a firm that was seeking a personnel assistant. If you constructed a functional resume, however, you could show how your ability to relate to people and to get along with individuals in all walks of life and in all levels of the business world would be useful in a field where you must gain the confidence of people and conduct in-depth interviews.

Functional Resume

BERNARD MYERS
1478 Lafayette Street
Chicago, Ill. 60627

(312) 555-6789

Position Objective

PRODUCTION MANAGER in a corporation, advertising agency or studio which offers a challenge to a creative problem-solver and requires a well-rounded knowledge of production.

Experience

Diversified background with advertising agencies, art studios and graphic arts firms as production manager, art director and general boardman.

Thorough knowledge of production from concept of visual layout and design to finished art ready for reproduction processing.

A creative problem-solver with full knowledge of all graphic arts supplies and materials and techniques of buying on the open market.

Familiar with all types of accounts, from consumer and specialty to heavy industrial. Account work has included electronic, bank, automotive, chemical, department store, utility, pharmaceutical, real estate, furniture and financial.

Have worked on annual reports, brochures, direct mail promotion, point-of-sale, publications, catalogs, visual aids, and all types of collateral material.

Thoroughly familiar with all printing processes, typography, mechanicals, silk screen, photo retouching, photography, packaging and label design.

Education

Rochester Institute of Technology   1961
Rochester, New York
B.S., Printing Technology

School of Visual Arts   1962
New York, N.Y.
Graphic Design

Employment History

Lawrence Arubian, Advertising Agency 418 Costagna Street Chicago, Ill.	Production Manager 10/76 - 10/78
Atlantic Advertising Agency 1422 S. LaSalle St. Chicago, Ill.	Production Manager 3/72 - 9/76
Sinclair Advertising Agency 27 S. Weymouth Avenue Springfield, Ill.	Assistant Art Director 9/71 - 2/72
Franklin Art Services, Inc. 4811 B Street Chicago, Ill.	Assistant Art Director 1/68 - 8/71
Roth Graphics, Inc. 825 Main St. Indianapolis, Ind.	Assistant Art Director 2/66 - 12/67
National Typefounders, Inc. 4805 N. Franklin St. Indianapolis, Ind.	Boardman 7/65 - 1/66
Commerce Poster Co. 87 Columbia Heights Chicago, Ill.	Boardman 9/64 - 5/65
Hardy & Roberts, Advertising 456 Littlejohn Road Chicago, Ill.	Layout Artist 7/62 - 8/64

Personal

Born: October 17, 1940

Willing to relocate

Married

Functional Resume

R E S U M E

ELLIOT A. LEWIS
325 Sheridan St.
Boston, Mass. 02115

(617) 948-3684

Sales Administrator

Customer Service Supervisor

Administrative Assistant

PROFESSIONAL HISTORY

Sales Administrator: Handled internal administration
for a group of sales representatives and customers
in a large consumer products company. Duties included
heavy phone work   and correspondence relating to
all types of customer service. Responsible for production information, customer complaints, reviewing
pricing and expediting of customer orders. I supervised a staff of 12 people handling liaison between
customers, sales force, warehouse and factory.

Operations and Sales: For a major coal producing
company, I analyzed sales and profit reports to determine profits formulas. I researched and gathered
data to develop trends on product lines for forecasting of sales in a competive market. I also studied
statistics of all supplies for both internal and customer use and furnished daily, weekly and monthly
tonnage reports for the use of management in maintaining quality standards and sales.

Administrative Assistant: As an assistant to the sales
manager of a leading appliance manufacturer, I helped
prepare cost studies for their product lines to determine pricing policies for existing and prospective
accounts. Prepared studies for sales force to aid
them in presenting price factors, quantity discounts,
special arrangements for warehousing and shipping.
Worked closely with the advertising department in
preparing sales promotion literature for the sales force.

EMPLOYMENT

1976 - 1980   Triton Sales Corporation
               Plymouth, Mass.
               Sales Analyst

83

1973 -1975   Foremost Packaging Company
             Boston, Mass.
             <u>Sales Administrator</u>

1960 - 1973 Alexander H. Sampson Coal Company
             Boston, Mass.
             <u>Sales Administrator</u>

1958 - 1960 International Electric Products Company
             Dedham, Mass.
             <u>Sales Correspondent</u>

1956 - 1958 New England Carpet Company
             Boston, Mass.
             <u>Sales and Order Department Assistant</u>

<u>EDUCATION</u>

Boston University
B.A.
Major - History
Minor - Business Management

<u>PERSONAL</u>

Age: 48
Married

Functional Resume

SANFORD F. STEWART

8641 Laramie Street   (312) 499-6805
Chicago, Ill. 60638

ADMINISTRATIVE SYSTEMS
MANAGEMENT

Profit oriented administrator with proven
record in management and information services,
including computer systems, reproduction, fac-
simile, supplies, records management, and microfilm. Innovative executive with expertise in
management consulting,methods and procedures,
feasibility studies, and EDP conversions.

ACHIEVEMENTS

- Effected $300,000 annual savings through 40%
  reduction in clerical staff by establishing centralized office services division in corporate
  headquarters with no reduction in departmental
  effectiveness.

- Increased productivity through EDP interface.
  Designed new input sources and forms, processing
  procedures, flow charts, data bases, and output
  reporting system.

- Reorganized and implemented new corporate inventory
  control system. Designed an improved purchasing
  procedures manual, effecting a net savings of
  ¢120,000 in one year.

- Supervised microfilm and COM programs for sales
  and marketing departments, corporate library and
  purchasing department. System produced substantial
  annual savings.

- Installed a centralized reproduction department which
  increased the overall efficiency of copy output
  throughout the firm and effecting a substantial
  savings in time and expense.

- Combined information resources, corporate libraries,
  technical, business and reference into single
  computerized information network for management and
  research.

- Installed a modern word-processing system, resulting
  in 25% reduction in clerical staff.

- Conducted feasibility studies for computer interface with existing manual systems.

- Upgraded corporate records retention systems. Saved $150,000 plus, reducing accumulated storage volume up to 50% by designing administrative comprehensive records management systems. Programs were expanded to include protection of vital records.

EMPLOYMENT

Nepco Mining & Minerals Corporation Manager, General Services	6/70 - 10/80	
Universal Oil Corporation Administrative Systems Manager	10/64 - 5/70	
Triton International Corporation Systems Supervisor	7/59 - 9/64	
Springfield Chemical Corporation Information Specialist	10/55 - 6/59	

EDUCATION

University of Chicago	MBA
University of Pennsylvania	B.S. Mathematics
Temple University	Programming

PROFESSIONAL
ASSOCIATIONS

American Management Association
American Federation of Information Processing Societies
Data Processing Management Association

PERSONAL

Born: October 17, 1930
Married
Will travel/relocate

Functional Resume

324 Renfrew Road	Office: (212) 461-3748
New Rochelle, N.Y. 10709	Home: (914) 684-3867

ADVERTISING PROMOTION EXECUTIVE

Strong marketing background plus award-winning
creativity to develop complex advertising and
sales promotional problems. Solid record of
achievements in package goods, including food,
cosmetics, drugs, plus excellent knowledge
of all phases of promotion, production and media.

ACCOMPLISHMENTS

Increased share of market for major cruise ship company
through a cooperative campaign with local travel agents throughout the country. Worked closely with advertising agency in
producing successful national television campaign which increased passenger volume by 22%.

Developed and implemented contest promotion which was responsible for capturing a major share of the business travel
market for a major airline.

Wrote a series of booklets on beauty and skin care for a
cosmetics company which was promoted successfully through
national magazines.

Developed a new advertising campaign for a fast-food chain
aimed at young families. As a result, business was increased
23% nationally.

Introduced first computerized microwave oven by unusual use
of 10-second TV spots to obtain maximum audience and frequency
at low cost. Result: record demand and sales.

Increased sales and volume for department store chain through
the creation of revolutionery in-store contest promotion.

Moved Golden Girl Shampoo to first position in sales by re-
directing strategy and concentrating on solving common hair
problems. New TV campaign evoked immediate positive consumer
response.

Conceived new product cateogry, wrote plan, devised creative
strategy for children's dentifrice.

Created an enlarged market for an ordinary dandruff shampoo
through a campaign designed to appeal to teenagers. Increased
awareness of the benefits of the product as the basis for
successful health-care coverage in national magazines.

87

Originated concept, created strategy plans for brand name
deodorant which turned an "adequate" market into a sustained pro-
fit-maker.

Responsible for establishing all marketing objectives and
strategies, determining all product positionings, developing
all copy direction for new product brought out by a major
cosmetics manufacturer.

As a consultant to a major chain of high fashion stores,
created an advertising campaign which increased traffic and
resulted in a 30% increase in sales revenue.

EMPLOYMENT HISTORY

Laramie Stores Corporation White Plains, N.Y.	1979	Consultant
Slade, Forrest & Hendrix, Inc. New York, N.Y.	1970 1976	Account Executive
North Atlantic Steamship Co. New York, N.Y.	1968 1970	Advertising Manager
Franklin Advertising Co. Newark, N.J.	1964 1968	Account Supervisor
Advanced Marketing Associates New York, N.Y.	1961 1962	Account Supervisor
White, Lipped & Trembling, Inc. New York, N.Y.	1959 1962	Account Executive

EDUCATION

State University of New York, Stony Brook, N.Y.
M.B.A., B.S., Marketing

PERSONAL

Born November 12, 1935
Married - will travel and relocate.

REFERENCES

John Harbon, President
North American Steamship Co.
26 Centre St.
New York, N.Y.

John Forrest, Vice President
Slade, Forrest & Hendrix, Inc.
576 Madison Avenue
New York, N.Y.

Jonathan Franklin, President
Franklin Advertising Co.
301 Butler St.
Newark, N.J.

Dr. Arnold Slivovity, President
Advanced Marketing, Inc.
408 Fifth Ave.
New York, N.Y.

Functional Resume

NAME: Rachael Butler

ADDRESS: 861 61st Avenue, Kansas City, Mo. 65039

TELEPHONE: (816) 684-3410

OBJECTIVE: To obtain a challenging position in personnel
              where I can effectively utilize my training
              and experience in the field of human relations.

EDUCATION: 1971   Master of Social Work
                      University of California
                      Davis, California

              1969   Bachelor of Arts
                      Kansas State University
                      Manhattan, Kansas

SUMMARY OF
EXPERIENCE: While with a major adoption service, I was
              involved in:

              * Directing and processing client intake program.

              * Interviewing and assessing clients.

              * Providing therapeutic counseling services
                to prospective parents.

              * Preparing and documenting investigative
                reports for the county courts.

              * Supervising a staff of administrative and
                clerical aids.

              As a member of the staff of a large city
              social service agency, I was responsible
              for:

              * Provision of diagnostic and therapeutic
                services to families experiencing stress or dis-
                ruption.

              * Marital and family counseling, both on a pre-
                ventive and crises-intervention basis.

ACHIEVEMENTS: Received promotions in all employment situations.
              Attained senior level position with correspond-
              ing authority and responsibility.

89

Successfully met defined goals within allotted time limits.

Established effective assessment approach in interviewing clients.

Developed leadership skills through attendance at seminars and workshops related to my occupation.

Achieved interpersonal skills to work effectively in a multi-racial environment.

EMPLOYMENT: January 1973 to September 1978

Childrens Aid Society
Topeka, Kansas
Adoption Counselor

November 1971 to January 1973

Kansas City Department of Social Services
Kansas City, Missouri
Social Worker

PERSONAL: Date of birth: May 2, 1948
Place of birth: St. Louis, Mo.
Height: 5'3"
Weight: 110 lbs.
Health: Excellent
Marital status: Single

SUMMARY: I believe my training, experience and aptitudes can be effectively utilized in the personnel field, and I am willing to undergo whatever transitional training which would be necessary to make me a potentially valuable asset in a corporate environment.

The Combination Resume

A merging of both the chronological and functional resumes is often the most effective. If you have a solid work record and are making a move in your own occupation, the combination resume is the best one to use.

You start with the same information as the first two resumes—personal identification and job objective. Then for at least half of the first page, write a condensed version of your background just as you would for the functional resume.

Following this, use the chronological form; dates, name of firm, description of duties, etc. See the samples on pages 71–78.

The Entry Level or Trainee Resume

If you are just out of school and looking for your first job or have had very light experience, your resume would have to be organized in a manner different from the chronological and functional forms.

The less experience you have, the harder it is to construct an effective resume. You have very little to say and a full page of white space in which to say it. Resist the temptation to fill it with trivia. However limited your experience and accomplishments, you can still organize and write an effective resume that will get you interviews.

First, list your personal data (as in the other resumes) followed by your job objective. At this stage in your life, you may not have a firm job objective—or you may be juggling three or four without knowing exactly what your objectives are. For the purposes of your resume, your objective should have some direction but be flexible.

Many trainees looking for their first job make the mistake of projecting their entire life's goals using job objective descriptions such as, "an entry level position with a large industrial firm that will lead to vice president" or, "to start at the bottom and work my way up to top management." These indicate a lack of maturity on the writer's part. At this point, it is much more effective to state as an objective, "entry-level position where I can utilize my education in finance and accounting and eventually make a contribution to a progressive employer" or "position as junior editor where I can develop my writing skills to their fullest extent."

After your job objective, go directly to your educational experience. You have little else to market. You do not have to be a college graduate. Whatever training or education you have had can be effectively developed in your resume.

If you have attended college, there is no need to list the name of your high school unless it offered a highly specialized curriculum such as art, science or printing.

Include the dates of your attendance, name and location of the school, college or university, and your degree (if any). Then indicate your major and minor subjects—but only if they are germane to your career objectives. Having a BA in history may qualify you to win prizes on a quiz show, but it won't particularly impress the personnel manager of a bank.

This is especially true if you majored in such subjects as Mandarin, Russian literature or dramatic arts. And please, spare your intended employers the information that you also took courses in yoga, belly dancing, camping, gourmet cooking or wine-making.

List any student organizations that you belonged to: professional fraternities, sororities, discussion groups—all educational-related activities. Your work on the school newspaper or magazine should particularly be mentioned.

After you have fully developed your educational background, go on to the experience section. Your work experience will at this time be negligible, but be sure to include any part-time or school experience.

The best school experience to list is an internship with a company involved in a work-study program with the college. This is becoming more common and is the best preparation for entry into the business world—as well as providing you with invaluable contacts. However, if you did not have access to this kind of a program, list any part-time jobs you had, no matter how trivial they might appear. Employers still retain some respect for young people who work—even partly—through college. Do not get too flowery in your description of these jobs. If you were a waiter or waitress there is no need to detail your ability to juggle eighteen cups and saucers simultaneously on your arm. If you were a baby sitter, forget the lecture on child rearing.

As for hobbies, the only time you should list your hobbies is when they have some bearing on your marketable skills or talents. A commercial artist whose hobbies are painting, bookbinding or photography should list them, as should a computer programmer who is also an electronics hobbyist. Your interest in macrame and skiing is admirable, but hardly of interest to an employer. Mentioning your great love of

hunting can hurt you. It may offend someone who is an avid environ-
mentalist.

At the end of your resume, under *miscellaneous,* indicate your date of
birth, marital status and availability for travel and/or relocation.

References are not necessary. At this stage, you don't have any references, and names of friends, relatives or college professors won't carry
much weight.

Combination Resume

856 Oceanview Place
Brooklyn, N.Y. 11628
(212) 555-7484

Resume

HENRY T. LAVERTY

Personnel Executive

SUMMARY OF QUALIFICATIONS   Extensive background in Personnel Administration with heavy experience in:

* Wage and salary administration
* Employee benefits and pensions
* Training and development programs
* Human relations
* Recruiting
* EEOC Practices
* OSHA Administration

Excellent verbal and written skills
Seasoned manager with proven supervisory ability to direct and motivate subordinates at all levels.

EDUCATION   M.B.A. – April 1961 – Columbia University Graduate School of Business Administration. Upper 25% of graduating class.

B.A. –Personnel – 1957 – Columbia University School of Arts and Science.

PROFESSIONAL EXPERIENCE

1971 to present   JOHNSON INTERNATIONAL CORPORATION
1160 Avenue of the Americas, New York, N.Y.

Director of Personnel for major manufacturer of electrical components with annual sales of $180 million.

Directed all phases of corporate personnel activities, heading department consisting of staff of 12.

Established recruitment procedures for exempt
and non-exempt personnel.

Supervised employee processing, including
orientation, training schedules and individual
counseling.

Developed and coordinated personnel policies
for dependent subsidiaries, devising forms,
manuals, guidelines and procedures.

Responsible for administering employee benefit
plans such as insurance, profit sharing, pensions. In charge of records, preparation of
government forms, reports and analyses for
ERISA. Evaluation of insurance reports and
distribution of deferred payments. Prepared
all forms and data for input to EDP installation.

Represented, with law department, corporate
management and beneficiaries in negotiations
of plans and dealings with insurers, attorneys,
and government agencies.

Originated employee literature to comply
with ERISA requirements and corporate benefit
plans.

Implemented annual EEOC reporting requirements. Analyzed contents, and made written
recommendations to management.

Provided administrative and advisory support
to director of labor relations in all matters
relating to union contracts and negotiations.
Sat on the committee and attended all meetings
with representatives of the work force and
labor unions.

Wrote job specifications to provide guidance
in hiring exempt and non-exempt personnel.

Administered employee programs, savings bond
purchases, tuition and educational grants,
recreational activities and merit awards.

1969 to 1972   DBA PUBLISHING COMPANY
                    528 Madison Avenue
                    New York, N.Y.

                    Personnel Manager in charge of all employment
                    activities for headquarters office of third
                    largest book publisher in the U.S. (2100 employees).

95

Developed a more efficient corporate recruiting program. Designed and implemented
orientation program, and employee skills
inventory profile. Conducted management
development and supervisory personnel
training sessions. Established and coordinated employee communication department and
edited external house organ. Prepared wage
and salary surveys and turnover analyses.

1963 to 1967   CONSOLIDATED FINANCE CO.
                 12 West 43rd St.
                 New York, N.Y. 10036

                 Assistant Personnel Manager - Developed re-
                 cruiting sources for 90 offices nationally.
                 Interviewed and selected employees for home
                 office.   Assisted in job evaluation, salary
                 administration and wage surveys. Prepared,
                 coordinated and conducted personnel training
                 and management development activities for all
                 offices.

1961 to 1963   NATIONAL OFFICE EQUIPMENT CO., INC.
                 48-26 Woodside Avenue
                 Long Island City, N.Y. 11345

                 Personnel Assistant - Gained experience in
                 personnel with major manufacturer of word
                 processing equipment in the following areas:
                 job evaluation, wage and salary studies and
                 administration, management training and devel-
                 opment, administration of pension and sick-
                 ness benefits, preparation of employee manuals
                 and recruiting brochures.

PERSONAL   Age: 44
                 Married
                 Willing to travel and relocate

AFFILIATIONS   American Society of Personnel Administrators
                 New York Personnel Management Association
                 National Association of Corporate Communicators

Combination Resume

R E S U M E

Rosalyn F. Brent
45 Terrace Avenue
Des Moines, Iowa 50310

(515) 561-3289

ARCHITECT/URBAN PLANNER/DESIGNER

BACKGROUND

Thirteen years of technical and administrative experience
in the field of urban planning and architecture. Developed
programs for the rehabilitation of decaying properties into
economically sound investments. Worked closely with government agencies, builders, investors and community organizations.
Coordinated and supervised the implementation of the design
and construction of a number of assigned projects, including
commercial properties, government buildings, housing and health
facilities.

EDUCATION

Ohio State University, Columbus, Ohio
B.S. Architecture

Drexel University, Philadelphia, Pa.
M.S. Urban Planning

HONORS

State of Ohio Urban Fellowship
Frank Perry Award for excellence in urban redevelopment design.

EXPERIENCE

Samuelson Associates, Des Moines, Iowa   Jan 1977 - Aug 1980
Project Coordinator
        Design and construction drawings for F.W. Woolworth's
        office in Chicago, Illinois...Rehabilitation of the
        Northwestern Housing Development Corporation in
        Newark, New Jersey...Proposal for the landscaping
        of terminal buildings at the new airport under construc-
        tion at Dayton, Ohio.

Lorraine Construction Co., Cedar Rapids, Iowa   Dec 1973 - Apr 1977
Project Manager
        Supervised design and construction drawings for the
        Fairfield Childrens' Center in Cedar Rapids...Reviewed
        activities by consultants, contractors and agencies to

assure conformance with established schedules...
Contract preparation, zone variance processing and
topographical mapping.

Northwest Construction Co., Cedar Rapids, Iowa   Jun 1971 - Sep 1973
Designer
           Assignments included presentation work, site planning,
           and construction drawings for a municipal library.

Fletcher Roberts Associates, Cedar Rapids, Iowa   May 1970 - Jun 1971
Designer, Planner
           Assignments included commercial buildings, shopping
           centers, interior designs, schools and high rise
           apartment buildings. Also, land use controls and the
           design and implementation of long-range planning programs.

Fremont, Patrick & Co., Chicago, Ill.   Mar 1966 -Apr 1970
Designer, Planner
           Assignments included design and planning analyses for
           hospital and health facility in Saudi Arabia.

Platt, Forrester & Levine, Chicago, Ill.   Feb 1965 - Jan 1966
Draftsman
           Construction drawings, model-making and checking
           buildings.

PERSONAL

           Age: 39
           Single
           Willing relocate in U.S. or overseas

Combination Resume

ROBERT A. RANSOM
332 S. W. 12th St.
Washington, D.C. 20019

(202) 555-6948

OBJECTIVE

To apply past educational knowledge and practical experience
in a responsible position in operations management, warehousing
and distribution of goods.

SUMMARY OF ACHIEVEMENTS

Ten years experience in all phases of shipping and receiving
. . .Established job responsibilities for 80 unionized employees resulting in increased production and efficiency of
operational systems. . . Restructured interstore transfer
procedures reducing internal shrinkage by 15%. . .Lowered
payroll costs by 20% while maintaining overall efficiency
of freight handling. . .Coordinated control of all paper flow
received and generated. . .Designed quality control standards
for shipments received. . .Increased average sales volume
15% by effective purchasing and inventory control methods.

EDUCATION

Washington & Lee University, Lexington, Va.   May 1968
Degree: Bachelor of Business Administration
Major: Finance
Minor: Economics

Columbia Community College, Washington, D.C.   Feb 1965
Degree: Associate in Arts and Science
Major: Retail Distribution

EMPLOYMENT

Hecht Stores, Inc.   July 1976
Washington, D.C.   Aug 1978

Position: Operations Management Coordinator

Responsibilities:
* Controlled all phases of incoming and outgoing freight and
  transfer operations.
* Routed all freight (soft and hard goods) to correct locality.
* Controlled flow of incoming and outgoing goods through
  efficient receiving and shipping scheduling.
* Controlled flow of all paperwork.
* Effectively managed staff of 80 employees by establishing
  job responsibilities.

99

Accomplishments

*   Restructured inter-store transfer system reducing internal shrinkage by 15% while decreasing labor costs.
*   Developed and modified system procedures lowering straight-time and overtime costs by 20%.
*   Restructured systems for control of all shipping.
*   Revised staff schedules to correspondent to high and low periods of operation.

Highway Department Stores, Inc.   Jun 1974
Lexington, Virginia   Jun 1976

Position: Hardgoods Warehouse Manager

Responsibilities:
*   Routed all incoming freight to correct locality.
*   Ordering and inventory control for 13 departments.
*   Application of inventory turnover ratios.
*   Supervised and controlled shipping and receiving documents.

Accomplishments

*   Reduced inventory resulting in a substantial saving.
*   Established route schedules for interstate transfers.
*   Established system of weekly inventory reports to improve ordering procedures.

Midway SuperSavers, Inc.   May 1968
Norfolk, Virginia   Jun 1974

Position: Assistant Store Manager

Responsibilities:
*   Purchasing and inventory control for 4 departments.
*   Routing incoming freight to correct locations.

Accomplishments

*   Effected inventory procedures which resulted in rapid turnover of goods.
*   Originated stockroom plans for 5 departments.
*   Handled vendor returns and condition markdowns.

PERSONAL

Date of birth: October 17, 1945
Marital status: Married
Height: 6'
Weight: 190 lbs.
Willing to travel

Combination Resume

VICTORIA J. NEILSON
7856 Kennedy Blvd.
Teaneck, N.J. 08693

(201) 541-3978

CREDIT MANAGER

Fully experienced in all aspects of credit management and
administration including account analysis and evaluation, cash
flow control, credit authorization, collections and administrative
supervision.

In-depth knowledge of all aspects of credit procedures in
consumer, industrial, wholesale and distributive credit
operations.

Profit-oriented with a thorough grasp of credit policies,
systems and procedures that has proved successful in increasing
cash flow and minimizing defaults. Familiar with computerized credit systems, EDP interface and applications.

Progressive career growth reflects ability to accept increasing
responsibilities.

PROFESSIONAL
EMPLOYMENT

1975 – 1981   American International Products Corporation
               220 Park Avenue
               New York, N.Y. 10016

               INTERNATIONAL CREDIT MANAGER in charge of credit
               operations for this billion dollar manufacturer
               of industrial, aerospace and building materials.
               Responsible for world wide administration of
               receivables. Company has 12 plants and sub-
               sidiaries in Europe and Latin America. Position
               requires familiarity with international finance,
               export credit and complex foreign exchange
               transactions.

               Past-due accounts were reduced by almost 30%
               through the development and implementation of
               collection procedures at local plant level.

1971 – 1975   National Office Products Corporation
               921 Lexington Avenue
               New York, N.Y. 10022

               CREDIT MANAGER responsible for account approval,
               receivables management, credit extension and
               collections for major manufacturer and distributor
               of typewriters, electronic calculators and office
               equipment, with more than 3500 active accounts.

Established and implemented current methods and
procedures which permits constant review of accounts.

Supervised staff of 15, and developed on-going
training and evaluation program, resulting in
reduced turnover.

1969 - 1971   Intercity Finance Co., Inc.
230 Park Ave.
New York, N.Y. 10020

ASSISTANT TO CREDIT MANAGER - Participated in all
aspects of consumer credit, including a major
expansion program.

Involved in credit investigation and approval.
Helped design new forms and procedures for more
rapid processing of credit applications.

EDUCATION   Farleigh Dickenson University
Teaneck, N.J.   1969
Bachelor of Science - Finance

ASSOCIATIONS

American Management Association
National Association of Credit Managers
Association of International Credit Executives

PERSONAL   Age: 35
Married
One child
Available for unlimited travel
Willing to relocate

REFERENCES   George Taylor, President
National Office Products Corporation
921 Lexington Ave.
New York, N.Y.

Jack Francis, Vice-President, Finance
American International Products, Inc.
220 Park Ave.
New York, N.Y.

Combination Resume

ALBERT RASKIN
1296 Second Ave.
New York, N.Y. 10022

(212) 520-6439

<u>ADVERTISING PRODUCTION MANAGER</u>
<u>PRINTING BUYER</u>

<u>BACKGROUND SUMMARY</u>

* Thorough knowledge of all phases of printing, typography, paper and binding.

* Estimating, procurement and quality control.

* Scheduling and traffic in all phases from receipt
of order through final delivery of job.

* Budget analysis and cost control.

* Approval and adjustment of supplier invoices.

* Personnel evaluation, hiring and termination.

* Client relations. Liaison between sales department,
suppliers, plant and customer.

<u>EXPERIENCE</u>

Maxwell Direct Mail Marketing Company   Aug 1975
888 Third Avenue   May 1978
New York, N.Y. 10022

<u>Production Manager</u>

Responsible for purchasing, production and traffic
of direct mail advertising and sales promotion
material with volume of $12 million annually.

Included were: magazines, books, broadsides, inserts,
folders, stationery and general advertising material,
black and white to 4-color process.

Frederick Peters Advertising, Inc.   Dec 1970
842 Park Avenue   Aug 1975
New York, N.Y. 10017

<u>Production Director</u>

Supervised a department of 8 assistants involved with
print production, traffic and client relations.

Edward J. Beyer, Advertising   Oct 1967
1440 Broadway   Dec 1970
New York, N.Y. 10001

Assistant Print Production Manager

Organized production department at new agency.
Assisted vice-president in traffic and production
activities of the agency.

Flash Printing Company   Jan 1962
23 Green Street   Oct 1967
New York, N.Y. 10004

Production Assistant

Handled all production details, made up job tickets,
scheduled presswork and delivery dates. Maintained
relations with customers, computed salesmen's com-
missions.

H.R.A. Advertising Associates   Apr 1959
34 Fifth Avenue   Jan 1962
New York, N.Y. 10016

Art & Production Trainee

Did pasteups and mechanicals, specified type and
generally assisted in all phases of graphic production.

EDUCATION

New York Employing Printers Association   1958
330 W. 34th St.
New York, N.Y.

High School of Printing   1959
New York, N.Y.

PERSONAL

Born: October 17, 1941
Married

Entry-level Resume

resume

Sheldon P. Barnard
126 Forrester St.
Philadelphia, Pa. 19115

Telephone: (215)232-4456

CAREER OBJECTIVE: A career in accounting or an accounting-
                    related field, with the opportunity to ad-
                    vance to a responsible position.

EDUCATION: Temple University
                    Philadelphia, Pa.
                    Bachelor of Business Administration - 5/81
                    Major: Accounting - 3.5 on 4.0 scale

                    Major subjects:
                    Auditing - Taxes
                    Accounting Theory - Advanced Taxes
                    Special areas (non-profit accounting)
                    Advanced Accounting (consolidations)

                    Minor subjects:
                    Business Law
                    Statistics
                    Computers
                    Corporate Finance
                    Money & Banking

SCHOLARSHIPS   Pennsylvania Merit Scholarship
HONORS: Dean's List (two semesters)

ACTIVITIES: Member, Business Students Association
                    Elected Dormitory Council Representative
                    Elected to Intramural Council
                    Captain of Intramural Football Team (2 years)
                    Member, Army Reserve Officers Training Corps

WORK EXPERIENCE: Member of the accounting staff for the
                    Temple Newspaper and Yearbook

                    Internship - 2 summers with Smith, French,
                    & Warwick, CPA's, Philadelphia, Pa.

                    Jr. Accountant - Vanguard Manufacturing
                    Company - 1 summer.

PERSONAL: Date of Birth: November 2, 1959
                    Marital Status: Single
                    Available for relocation

Entry-level Resume

SELMA MARKSON
673 Silver Road
Northport, L.I., N.Y. 11763
(516) 555-2345

EMPLOYMENT
OBJECTIVE: A responsible entry level position in marketing,
               leading to product management responsibilities.

EDUCATION: Master of Business Administration 1979 - 1981
               Pennsylvania State University
               Major: Marketing

               Master's degree field project:
               Conducted a survey of regional marketing factors
               for a nationally known consumer product package
               goods manufacturer. Analysis focused on regional
               variations in share of market.

               Evaluated sales promotion strategies to determine
               optimal approach in motivating wholesalers and
               dealers. Designed a mail survey and subsequent
               data analysis to determine consumer attitudes
               toward the product and its competitors.

               Bachelor of Science   1974 - 1978
               Indiana State University
               Major: Economics

EXPERIENCE: National Bank of United States   1972 - 1974
               34 W. 92nd St.
               New York, N.Y. 10023

               Assistant to Loan Officer - Submitted recommenda-
               tions on installment loan applications. Advised
               customers on available financing arrangements.
               Maintained customer accounts, prepared over-
               draft reports.

               G.A.P. Building Corporation
               Forest Hills, N.Y.

               Employed three summers during college as Assistant
               to Construction Foreman.

ACTIVITIES: National Foundation - Active volunteer for local
               chapter of March of Dimes. Organized and participated
               in a community education and fund raising program.

PERSONAL   Age 26
DATA: Single
               Available immediately

REFERENCE: John Casandra, Assistant Vice President
               National Bank of the U.S.
               34 W. 92nd Street
               New York, N.Y. 10023

Entry-level Resume

Harold Roberts
1694 Clay Avenue
Bronx, N.Y. 10451
(212) 861-4389

JOB OBJECTIVE

To become a member of an accounting staff, with an
opportunity for further advancement in the organization. To continue my education and eventually
become a Certified Public Accountant.

EDUCATIONAL BACKGROUND

The Bernard M. Baruch College of the City University
of New York.
Degree: Bachelor of Business Administration - June 1981
Major: Accounting
Activities: Member of Accounting Society

PART-TIME AND SUMMER EXPERIENCE

Edward Brodsky, C.P.A.
226 W.34th St.
New York, N.Y. 10001   2/81 - 6/81

Duties: Assisted in the preparation of financial
statements, recording of transactions, posting to
general ledger, bank reconciliations, and preparation
of tax returns.

Department of Tax Collection, City of New York
80 Lafayette St.
New York, N.Y.   8/60 - 8/80

Duties: Prepared estimated claims in connection with
bankruptcy matters.

Department of Tax Collection, City of New York
80 Lafayette St.
New York, N.Y.   6/79 - 8/79

Finance Department, City of New York
40 Church St.
New York, N.Y.   6/78 - 8/78

Duties: Processed income tax returns for billing, refunds,
and quality control procedures.

PERSONAL DATA

Marital Status- Single
Date of birth - October 17, 1958
Willing to travel and relocate

Entry-level Resume

RUTH M. PETROV   Age: 22
1725 Sedgewick Ave.   Height: 5'1"
Bryn Mawr, Pa. 19203   Weight: 105 lbs
                                                    Single

(215) 798-6473

PROFESSIONAL OBJECTIVE:

    To obtain an entry-level position in the Personnel
Department of a company which would afford an opportunity for growing responsibility and advancement.

EDUCATION:

    Bachelor of Science   June, 1981
Temple University
Major: Personnel Management

COURSES OF SPECIAL INTEREST

    Management of Human Resources
Compensation of Human Resources
Industrial Psychology
Employment of Human Resources
Labor Relations
Development of Human Resources
Psychology of Human Factors
Wage and Salary Administration
Operations Management in the Personnel Department
Special Study Project: "Experiential Learning in
Personnel and Management."

EXTRACURRICULAR ACTIVITIES:

    Activities President, Personnel Management Council
Vice President, Phi Chi Theta
Selected for Discussion Leader
Service awards for Business Student Council

EXPERIENCE:

    September 1977 to May 1980
Summers and Part-time
Bursars Office
Temple University

PERSONAL:

    Age: 22
Height: 5'1"
Weight: 105 lbs.
Marital status: Single

Entry-level Resume

LEONARD HEWITT   (203) 846-9206
1475 Walton Ave.
Stamford, Conn. 06604

OBJECTIVE: To become associated with a firm as a Computer
              Programmer and to advance into a career in
              data management systems.

EDUCATION: University of Connecticut
              Bachelor of Science, 1978
              Major: Computer Science - 2nd major: Business

              Computer Related Courses   Business Related Courses
              Computer Languages   Principles of Management
              COBOL Programming   Business Policy
              FORTRAN Programming   Introduction to Statistics
              Computer Structures   Financial Analysis
              Data Structures   Financial Accounting
              Artificial Intelligence   Business Economics
              Basic Programming   Mathematics

EXPERIENCE: Interstate Computer Corporation
              Stamford, Connecticut
              Four years summer experience

              1976 and 1977   General office assistant
              1977 and 1978   Programmer Trainee
              1979 and 1980   Assistant Programmer

              STUDENT HOUSING at University of Connecticut.
              Three semesters as a "Student Manager", pro-
              viding experience of managing small apartment
              building and coordinating activities in the
              surrounding community.

              FOOD SERVICE
              Four years of part-time experience at the
              campus dining hall.

              FINANCIAL ASSISTANCE DEPARTMENT
              School of Business
              University of Connecticut
              Part-time experience working with the DEC-10
              Computing System at the University data processing
              facility. In this position, I learned a great
              deal about the latest mini-computer system and
              its applications.

PERSONAL: 22 years old
              6'1"
              168 lbs.
              Single

REFERENCES: University of Connecticut
              Placement Office
              Stamford, Connecticut

Resume for Retired Job Applicants

<u>FRANK R. BLAISE, JR.</u>

1657 Orange Court
Dallas, Texas 76070

Phone: 214-766-5554
_____

OBJECTIVE: To obtain a position which would utilize my many
years of experience and expertise in the personnel
or security field.

PROFESSIONAL
BACKGROUND: 1965 - 1980   Southwest Chemical Corporation,
Dallas, Texas

POSITION: Chief of Security Services

Established a comprehensive system of plant and
office secufity for 25,000 employees in 4 manufacturing plants.

Worked closely with the Department of Defense
of the U.S. Government in the issuance of clear-
ance for employees involved in the use of classified
documents and equipment.

Conducted investigations of criminal actions
against the company, and appeared as witness in
cases brought to trial.

Developed a reporting system to keep upper level
management apprised of all security activities
throughout the company facilities.

Maintained closs relationship with federal and
local law enforcement agencies to coordinate investigations of criminal activity against the firm.

Conducted seminars for management and employee
groups on the subject of internal security matters.

Coordinated the security activities of four
plants located in the southwest by frequant
visits and contact with security officers in other
facilities.

Was responsible for employment of uniformed security personnel on the company premises and took
part in salary negotiations with applicable unions
representing these employees.

1955 - 1965

POSITION: Director of Personnel

Responsibilities included recruiting, interviewing
and hiring executive personnel for home office
staff.

Frank R. Blaise, Jr.

Administered the personnel department and supervised all phases of employment procedures for exampt
and non-exempt personnel.

Established wage and salary standards for plant
and office personnel for heaquarters facility.

Supervised the maintenance of all personnel
records and files.

Represented margement as part of the negotia-
tion team in contract talks with participating
labor unions.

Prior to 1955

POSITION: Personnel Assistant

EDUCATION: University of Alabama: Industrial Psychology

University of Texas: Industrial Relations

Federal Bureau of Investigation, Washing, D.C.
  Industrial Security Procedures

U.S. Army Military Police School - Ft. Riley,
  Kansas

PROFESSIONAL
AFFILIATIONS: Police Chiefs Association of Texas

American Society for Industrial Security

Security Officers Association of Texas

American Society of Training and Development

American Society of Personnel Administration

MISCELLANEOUS: Age: 58

Married

Retired from Southwest Chemical Corporation

Willing to relocate and perform limited travel

Review Your Resume Periodically

After your resume is written and used a few times, try to evaluate its effectiveness. Is it getting you a sufficient number of interviews? Is it getting any interviews at all? If you feel it is lacking something, try to analyze and rewrite it. It's not cast in bronze.

A lot of job-hunters continue to use the same resume, reprinting it over and over again when it is obviously not doing the job.

Even after you have gotten a job and no longer need it, keep it handy anyway and update it annually. It will help you to take stock of yourself, and you never know when you may want it in a hurry.

Resume Preparation Form

A document as important as your resume should not be started without a great deal of preliminary thought and planning.

Before you put a single page into your typewriter, you should have before you a complete dossier of your background, with information organized in a way that will not only make writing your resume easier, but will insure your having included all the material that should be there.

One reason that people have difficulty in composing a resume is because the only preparation they make is taking the cover off the typewriter. The compulsion to start writing immediately without adequate preparation causes most of the difficulty.

The following pages contain a step-by-step form which when properly completed will provide the input for your resume. Fill it out as neatly and completely as possible.

RESUME PREPARATION FORM

Full name:_____

Address:_____

Telephone (area code):_____
                         (home)   (business)

Objective or job title: (List several, and choose the most
                         appropriate before finally drafting the
                         resume)

_____   _____

_____   _____

_____   _____

Summary of experience and background: (A short paragraph describ-
                         ing in general terms, your work exper-
                         ience and qualifications)

_____

_____

_____

_____

_____

_____

_____

Education and Training:

High school :_____
(list only if not a college graduate, or if it offered a specialized curriculum or was a trade school)

College or university:_____

Dates of attendance_____Degree:_____

Major area of studies:_____

Minor area of studies:_____

Grades:_____
        (Major subject: average)   (Overall average)

113

Extracurricular activities:
(fraternities, soriorities, professional organizations, study clubs, etc.)

_____

_____

_____

Work-study activities:
(internships, staff positions at college)

_____

_____

* *

(THE WORK EXPERIENCE SECTION BELOW, SHOULD BE COMPLETED FOR EACH POSITION YOU HAVE HELD.)
(List your last position first)

Dates of employment: (month & year)_____

Most recent title:_____

Name & address of firm:_____

Products or services:_____

Brief description of your duties and responsibilities:

_____

_____

_____

_____

_____

Accomplishments: (specific achievements you can point to, such as cost savings, improved systems, contributions to your department or profit picture.)

_____

_____

_____

_____

_____

114

Promotions, Awards, Citations: _____

_____

_____

_____

Miscellaneous: (Professional organizations, trade associations, business clubs and other job related memberships.)

_____   _____

_____   _____

(THE ABOVE WORK EXPERIENCE SECTION SHOULD BE DUPLICATED FOR EACH JOB)
* *

Age: (date of birth or years)_____

Travel or relocation preferences:_____

Optional information:(references, marital status, military experience) _____

_____

_____

_____

_____

_____

_____

_____

Resume Action Words

A

activated
actuated
addressed
administered
analyzed
arranged
assembled
assisted
attracted
authored

C

charted
closed up
collected
compiled
completed
composed
conceived
concluded
conducted
confined
constructed
contracted
contributed
controlled
coordinated
corrected
created

D

decreased
demonstrated
designed
determined
developed
devised
diagrammed
directed
disciplined
discovered
disseminated
distributed
documented
doubled

E

edited
eliminated
enhanced
enlarged
established
exceeded
executed
expanded
expedited

F

facilitated
forecasted
formulated

G

guided

H

headed

I

illuminated
illustrated
implemented
improved
increased
initiated
innovated
installed
instituted
introduced
invented
investigated

L

launched

M

managed
maximized
minimized
modernized
modified
motivated

N

negotiated

O

obtained
operated
optimized
organized
originated
overhauled

P

performed
planned
prepared
procured
promoted
proposed
provided
put together

R

reconciled
recorded
recruited
reduced
refined
renewed
replaced
reported
researched
responsible for
reviewed
revised
revitalized

S

safeguarded
secured
shut down
simplified
slashed
sold
solved
sparked
staffed
started
stimulated
summarized
supervised
synthesized
systematized

T

terminated
took charge
took over
trained
transacted
triggered

U

upgraded

V

verified

13

Letters
For All Occasions

In any discussion of job-hunting, it is the resume that usually gets all the attention. Equally important, however, are the letters that you have to write during each phase of your job campaign.

The most important letter you will have to write is the cover letter to accompany your resume. But there are others you should know how to write if you want to get the most out of your efforts to find a job.

On the following pages you will find samples of these letters. You may not need all of them, but certain ones, such as resume cover letters and thank-you letters, are mandatory.

By using these examples as a guide, you should be able to construct your own letters to fit your particular circumstances.

Be sure to keep track of all the letters and resumes you send out. (See the form on page 135.)

Marlene Frenkel
1418 Euclid Avenue
Cleveland, Ohio 44128

October 18, 1980

Advertiser
Box 1826
Cleveland Plain Dealer
Cleveland, Ohio 44111

Gentlemen:

Your advertisement for a full-charge bookkeeper in the October 18th issue of the Cleveland
Plain Dealer seems to fit my background exactly.

As you can see in the enclosed resume, I have
had 14 years experience as a bookkeeper with both
large and small firms, and I am completely familiar
with all operations through the general ledger.
I have also had experience with computerized payroll
procedures.

Since I believe I have the general qualifications you are seeking, I would appreciate the opportunity of an interview.

Sincerely yours,

Marlene Frenkel

426 Main St.
Cherry Hill, N.J. 07406
December 26, 1980

(609) 851-9587

Box 2694
THE JOURNAL OF ENGINEERING
1681 Avenue of the Americas
New York, N.Y. 10020

Dear Sir:

The enclosed resume is submitted
in response to your advertisement for
a Structural Engineer, in Philadelphia.

I am a Professional Engineer with
heavy experience in the design and utilization of precast-prestressed concrete.
My employer is moving to plant facilities
in the Los Angeles area and I do not
wish to relocate at this time. My present salary is $22,000 per year.

I hope to have the opportunity of
presenting my qualifications in a personal
interview.

Sincerely yours,

Bernard A. Berman

Mary Ann Nudnick
146 Cherry St.
Peekskill, N.Y. 12972

November 1, 1980

Ms. Lorraine Peterson
Personnel Director
Cosmopolitan Insurance Co.
62-16   68th Ave.
Forest Hills, N.Y. 11243

Dear Ms. Peterson:

I have just graduated from Columbia University with a Bachelor of Science degree in Mathematics, and I am seeking a position as an actuarial trainee.

Although I have no working experience except for miscellaneous summer employment while in school, I can offer hard work, enthusiasm and a desire to succeed in return for an opportunity with your firm.

I am enclosing a resume for your consideration, and would appreciate the opportunity of an interview.

Yours very truly,

Mary Ann Nudnick

October 17, 1980

Box X-2567
The New York Times Bldg.
New York Times
250 W. 43rd St.
New York, N.Y. 10036

<u>Consumer Affairs Representative</u>

Gentlemen:

Your advertisement in the October 16th issue of the New York Times fits my background exactly.

For the past 6 years I have been in the public relations department of a major pharmaceutical firm, and am presently in charge of all customer relations and consumer affairs activities.

In this capacity, I write and help produce all of the company's communications which are designed to improve relations between the firm, the nearby community and consumers of the company's products. This includes pamphlets, brochures, speeches, publicity releases and correspondence.

I am 32 years old, have a degree in journalism, and am available for immediate employment.

Since my experience seems to fit the requirements of your positon, I would appreciate the opportunity of an interview.

Yours truly,

Barbara Williams

1494 Drake Avenue
New York, N.Y. 10012

(212) 694-4321

FRANCINE HOPKINS
4286   9th Street
San Francisco, Calif. 93102

(415) 968-4325

December 18, 1980

Mr. Allen Forbes, Design Director
Blue Grass Textile Company
20 Hoxey Street
San Francisco, Calif. 92513

Dear Mr. Forbes:

I am textile designer waiting to
be discovered.

I cannot offer you experience, but
I do have a Bachelor of Fine Arts degree
in Textile Technology from the University
of California, and I have been told by
my instructors and certain biased relatives
that I do have some talent.

Since your firm is recognized as a
leader in the production of a wide variety
of domestic and other textile products
for home and industry, I would like very
much to be considered for a junior art
now or in the near future.

I would appreciate the opportunity of
bringing in my portfolio for your appraisal
and consideration.

Sincerely yours,

Francine Hopkins

Frank Greenspan
41 Archer Drive
Norfolk, Va. 24557

(703) 848-2457

Mr. George Miles, V.P.
Southland National Bank
15 Main Street
Norfolk, Va. 24561

Dear Mr. Miles:

I am a commercial loan officer with eight
years of banking experience.

Because my present employer is a small organization with very limited opportunity for
growth, I am seeking a position which will enable
me to use my experience and knowledge to its fullest advantage. As a recognized leader in the
field of commercial banking, your organization
is the kind of firm I would like to be associated
with.

I have a B.A. degree in finance from the
University of Pennsylvania and an M.B.A. from the
Wharton School of Finance. My experience includes two years as a financial analyst and four
years as a commercial loan officer. I am thoroughly
familiar with all phases of commercial banking
operations.

I would welcome the opportunity of meeting
with you or one of your staff to present details
of my education and experience, and would be
happy to submit my resume for your consideration.

Yours very truly,

FRANK GREENSPAN

```
            FRANCIS O'BRIEN
            840 Main Street
         Louisville, Ky 40223




                              November 25, 1980




Dear Jim:

     Just as everything seemed to be going
so well in my job, the roof fell in.  Last
week, the company announced it was clos-
ing its Louisville branch office.  This
sudden and unexpected development means
that I am now back on the job market.

     I have already lined up a couple of
interviews here in town, but knowing how
uncertain job hunting can be, I can use
all the contacts I can get.

     You know my record as a salesman.
If you hear of any possibilities in your
travels, I would certainly appreciate
hearing about them.

     As soon as I rewrite my resume, I
will send you a copy to bring you up to
date on my recent activities.

                    Cordially,
```

2631 Franklin St.
E. Northport, N.Y.
April 9, 1981

(516) 345-6678

Mr. Manuel Ortiz
Managing Editor
"Latin American Business"
1 World Trade Center
New York, N.Y. 10004

Dear Manny:

At the last luncheon meeting
of the Export Club, I mentioned to you
that I was resigning from Bradford &
Company. You were kind enough to offer
your help in finding a new connection.

To familiarize you with details of
my background, I am enclosing a copy
of my resume. As I told you at the
meeting, I would be particularly interested in becoming associated with a firm
doing business in Central and South America,
where I could use my international
marketing background and language skills.

Any contacts you can generate as
editor of the leading trade magagine
in the field of Latin American commerce,
would be very much appreciated.

Cordially,

Lawrence Cogen

```
                    JACK LITTLE
                  4816 N. 8th Street
                Philadelphia, Pa. 19007


                                    November 17, 1980


Mr. Henry Thorenson
Executive Vice President
Penn Industrial Corp.
1816 J.F. K. Boulevard
Philadelphia, Pa. 19023

Dear Mr. Thorenson:

     As you know, my present firm, National
Oronoco Corporation, has merged with the Mid-
Atlantic Corporation, and as a result my position
as Purchasing Manager  has been eliminated.

     As you can see by the enclosed resume, my
background in purchasing includes over 10 years
of diversified managerial experience. Through
purchasing procedures which I originated and
implemented, I have been responsible for savings
upwards of $300,000 annually for my present
employer.

     Since Penn Industrial is a leading firm in
the industrial equipment field, I would like to
be considered for a position in either your pur-
chasing or operations department, and I would
appreciate the opportunity of meeting with you to
discuss this possibility.

     Your consideration is very much appreciated.

                         Sincerely yours,


                         JACK LITTLE
```

MARK N. PATRINO
4215 Farrar St.
Chicago, Illinois 60617

December 22, 1980

Mr. James Bozell
Creative Director
French, Rodney & Forrester, Inc.
215 S. LaSalle St.
Chicago, Ill. 60606

Dear Mr. Bozell:

The enclosed article regarding your promotion appeared in this week's edition of Advertising Age. May I offer my congratulations?

Since the article also mentions the acquisition of several new accounts by your agency, I am wondering whether you contemplate increasing your staff to service this new business. If so, I would very much like to be considered for a position on your art staff.

I am presently Assistant Art Director for a major 4A agency, assigned to two large package goods accounts. I have won a number of awards for my work, and I would like to show my portfolio and reels to you at your convenience.

If there is nothing available at this time, I would appreciate your accepting my resume for any possibilities in the future.

With all best wishes in your new position, I am

Sincerely yours,

Mark N. Patrino

MIRIAM CONNORS
1984 Crescent Street
Atlanta, Georgia 31221

November 12, 1980

Ms. Cynthia Nelson
Atlanta Personnel Agency
1223 Peachtree Street
Atlanta, Ga. 31201

Dear Ms. Nelson:

This is to advise you that I am no
longer available for a position and therefore request that you remove my application
from your active files.

Although I did not get a position through
your agency, it certainly was not for lack
of effort on your part.

You were very helpful in many ways,
and your courtesy and personal interest
are very much appreciated.

You can be sure I shall recommend your
firm to any individuals or companies who may
be interested in agency service.

Sincerely yours,

Miriam Connors

MARTHA LAMPIER
426 S. 4th Avenue
Dover, Delaware

December 16, 1980

Mr. Samuel Jackson
Arlington Publishing Co.
249 Main St.
Dover, Delaware 18901

Dear Mr. Jackson:

    Thank you for giving me the opportunity
of presenting my qualifications for the position of Marketing Trainee.

    I am very much interested in the job and
was especially impressed with the information
you provided about the future of the company
and the potential of the position.

    As I explained, my goal is to achieve a
successful career in corporate marketing, and
from what you told me about the position, I
believe I can do the job well and eventually
make a real contribution to your marketing
programs.

    Your favorable consideration will be
appreciated.

                    Sincerely yours,

                    Martha Lampier

ELLIOT T. HAYWARD
41-86 Dinwood St.
New Orleans, La.70123

October 17, 1981

Mr. Robert Miles
International Marketing Mgr.
Pan American Oil Corp.
1271 Liberty St.
New Orleans, La. 72480

Dear Bob:

The letter of refernce you were kind
enough to provide my new employer was, I am
told, the deciding factor in my being offered
the job. Your prompt and generous words are
very much appreciated.

My new position as Assistant Marketing
Manager with the Southeast Mining Co., is
exactly the kind of job I was seeking,
and I look forward to a long and happy association with this fine firm.

I expect to be at the next meeting of
the Marketing Club in November and I hope
to have the opportunity of meeting you there.

Sincerely,

Elliot T. Hayward

4805 N. Franklin St.
Philadelphia, Pa. 19460

March 28, 1981

Mr. Jim D'Amato
Raleigh Employment Agency
1630 Broadway
New York, N.Y. 10020

Dear Jim:

As you know I accepted a position with Ace Manufacturing Company, and I will be starting with them on August 26th at a salary of $19,500.

It is just the kind of spot I have been looking for, and I thank you for your efforts in placing me there. I am particularly grateful for your going to bat for me in negotiating the higher salary.

Again, my sincere thanks for your help.

Cordially,

Harold Brodsky

Paul Jackson
1475 Grand Street
Pittsburgh, Pa. 17261

July 14, 1981

Mr. Herman Corcoran, Director
National Assn. of Personnel Mgrs.
86 Morgan Avenue
Pittsburgh, Pa. 17842

Dear Mr. Corcoran:

    I want to express my appreciation to
your organization for the assistance given
me in my job campaign. Your aid was instrumental in my getting two job offers, one of
which I have just accepted.

    Your seminar "Preparing For the Interview,"
was particularly helpful, and contributed
greatly to my success in finding a job. Every
member of your staff connected with the job-aid
program showed courtesy and understanding,
presenting your program in a most salutory
manner.

    Again, thanks for your help.

                    Sincerely,

                    PAUL JACKSON

JACQUELINE RATNER
1422 North 8th Street
New Rochelle, N.Y. 13581

                                    September 16, 1981

Florence Lerner
156 W. 96th Street
New York, N.Y. 10023

Dear Florence:

    I am happy to report that I have just
gotten a new job, and I want to thank you
for all of your help.

    I contacted some of the people you
recommended and although my job is not
with one of them, your introductions did
help me get extra interviews.

    Your kindness in extending your time
and effort on my behalf is very much appreciated. I hope we can get together
for lunch someday soon, where I can thank
you personally.

                        Cordially,

                        Jacqui Ratner

14

Resume Control Form

Complete this form whenever you send a resume or a letter to a company. It will help you keep track of your resumes for follow-up.

Date	Name and address of company	Officer and title	Position and source	REMARKS: Response, follow-up, etc.

15

How to Survive the Interview

Everything you have done up to now—research, preparation, writing your resumes and cover letters, developing direct mail lists and all of the other time-consuming details—has had one single objective: to get interviews. This is where the main action takes place. It is also the place where competent, qualified job hunters with excellent credentials and good qualifications destroy themselves in a matter of minutes—not because they are wrong for the job, but because of carelessness, lack of knowing some of the basic rules of interviewing and unpreparedness, all of which could have been avoided. Too many applicants go into an interview without the faintest notion of what they are going to say, expecting to play it by ear. They usually fall flat on their faces.

This chapter tells you how to avoid the pitfalls and traps of an interview—what information to go in with, how to answer the easy questions and field the tough ones—how to handle the salary situation—what kind of interviews to expect—when to talk and when to keep quiet—how to dress for an interview and what to do after the interview.

All of it has been said before, but in today's competitive market, it cannot be repeated too often.

The Key Questions

After sifting through the volumes of published material about interviews, and ploughing through all the psychological jargon on depth interviews, stress interviews, patterned interviews, guided and unguided interviews and a host of other techniques and systems, it all boils down to three major questions: (1) Do you have the qualifications for the job? (2) Can you convince your interviewer that you have the qualifications? (3) Does the interviewer like you? The last item figures very heavily in the final decision.

John T., who is a personnel recruiter for a major electronics firm, confessed to me that very early in the interview he gets a distinct positive or negative feeling about the applicant sitting across from him which influences the rest of the interview. Regardless of qualifications, if the vibrations are positive the interview flows smoothly. If not, he finds it increasingly difficult to maintain interest.

This may seem unfair and arbitrary, but it would be naive to say that personal bias does not creep into every interview to some degree, just as it does with any relationship. Very few of us can be completely objective in dealing with people.

If this is the case, then why all the talk about preparation? If it is simply a matter of chemistry, why not just go in and ad lib it? Simply stated, the way you present yourself will establish the atmosphere of the interview. That and the amount of preparation you have done, plus the way you handle yourself, will add up to the vital first impression. If it all comes together, you've got an edge on the job. If it doesn't, you may have also made your last impression.

Look Your Best

A few words about appearance. It should not really be necessary to mention this at all, but from where I sit in the interviewer's chair, I am often appalled at the variety and style of clothing worn by men and women looking for jobs. Granted that today's acceptable standards of dress are far more liberal than they once were, it is still necessary to conform to some standard of taste. The days of white shirt, grey flannel suits and wing-tip shoes are long gone, but the business world has not completely capitulated to blue jeans, cowboy boots and navy pea coats. A man should wear a suit, plain shirt and subdued tie at an interview; a woman should wear a dress, skirt and blouse, or pants suit—at least for the interview. Once you get the job, working attire becomes more casual.

Remember, you will probably have your first interview with someone in the personnel department. These people usually evaluate appearance before anything else. If you do not pass this test, you may never get a chance to present more substantial qualifications to higher officials in the firm. There are some exceptions, of course, but they usually apply to people in highly creative occupations—and generally not to entry levels. Certain advertising agencies, publishers and art studios, for instance, would not panic if an artist or writer came in wearing blue jeans and sneakers, so long as he or she has been successful at the particular craft.

But—if you are a beginner, creative or not, don't try it. You won't get past the reception desk. As a neophyte artist or writer, you had better look like an accountant or a stockbroker on your first interview.

Preparation for the Interview

Successful interviews, those leading to job offers, are no accident. Regardless of the influence of personal bias, discussed earlier, lots of homework is required of the applicant who gets the job. Preparation consists of three elements: (1) knowledge of the job specifications, duties and responsibilities, (2) knowledge of the qualifications—both educational and experiential, and (3) knowledge of the company.

Knowing the specifications. It is not always easy to have full knowledge of the job specifications. This is especially true if you are being interviewed as the result of answering a classified advertisement, since these usually contain little information about the job. If, however, you are referred by an employment agency, a recruiter or some other third party, you can get the information you need if you are willing to dig for it.

Employment agencies are in a position to obtain job specifications in great detail—if they go after them, and are not too lazy to offer them to the applicant. Many agency counselors do not get the full specifications of the job and some who have them fail, in their anxiety to refer you out to the client, to give you what they have. It's up to you to insist on getting them. And don't be afraid of antagonizing the counselor. If you are a placeable applicant, you can get all the information you want by insisting upon it. When you know exactly what a job requires, you are in a position to emphasize your strengths to the interviewer.

A thorough interview often turns into a near-adversary proceeding. Like a prosecutor cross-examining a witness, an interviewer will try to zero in on your weaknesses and it is up to you to field the questions in order to give the most positive picture of yourself. The more you know about the job requirements, the better you will be able to handle this situation.

Knowing the Company. This is the most important preparation you can do. With good sources available for this research, there is no excuse for anyone to go into an interview not armed with facts about a company. Start with the business section of your public library. A list of appropriate directories and publications are shown on pages 177–178. And don't forget to look at the company's annual report. You can easily get one from almost any company just by calling them up and asking that it be sent to you. It usually gives lots more than just balance sheets.

If you are a senior just graduating from college, your school placement office probably has booklets and other material prepared by companies for recruiting purposes. These publications contain detailed information about a firm, including benefits, promotion procedures and complete organizational data. An excellent source for data on a corporation is a brokerage office. In addition to annual reports, brokerage firms are depositories of a lot of corporate information, and many have libraries that can be used on request. From these sources, you can obtain information such as:

> volume of business
> number of employees
> location of plants
> names of subsidiaries and divisions
> products and services
> growth pattern and potential
> future prospects
> markets
> name and titles of executives and managers
> financial information

These are basic facts you should know before going into an interview. The material is available. It's up to you to get it.

Be on Time

The first rule of the interview, and one which is inviolate, is promptness. If you are late, you had better have a pretty good excuse, such as your bus being hijacked. Being on time means being about ten minutes early, not to impress the interviewer, but to give yourself time to relax, get accustomed to the surroundings and mentally review some of your facts.

What kind of interview can you expect? You won't know until it starts. There are almost as many variations of interviews as there are interviewers. The majority fall into three classifications: the guided interview, the unguided interview and the stress interview.

As the name implies, the guided interview is conducted along formal lines, the interviewer asking questions in a planned sequence. The interviewer literally works from a check list, deviating very little from standard procedure. This kind of direct questioning does not give you much opportunity to expand on your answers. The way to handle this kind of interview is to not allow the interviewer to cut you short. Take a reasonable amount of time to answer each question, even if the question is designed for a yes or no response.

The unguided or unstructured interview lets you carry the ball for a good part of the time. The interviewer gives you general subjects to discuss rather than specific questions to answer. You may think the unguided interview would give you a better opportunity to sell yourself, but watch out. It can backfire. Having the chance to speak freely about yourself with little interruption gives you an excellent opportunity to plant both feet firmly in your mouth.

This happens rather often. One particular case comes to mind. Bernard C. was referred by me to a large insurance company for a position as a management trainee. The personnel manager, a practitioner of the unguided interview technique, invited the applicant to talk about himself. It was discovered early in the interview that they had both attended the same university and had mutual acquaintances among the faculty. This led to a free-for-all discussion in which the applicant, eager to impress his listener with his sophistication, admitted to a number of indiscretions at college, including an off-campus arrest.

End of interview.

Don't allow yourself to fall into this kind of trap, which is sometimes purposely set in an unguided interview. If asked to discuss yourself and your background, ask your interviewer the aspect of your background in which he is particularly interested. Keep to the point. Give pertinent information about your previous jobs, education and training. Just state the facts. Do not get into personality discussions, rating the performances of fellow employees or supervisors. And never, never criticize a former employer. He may have been the biggest s.o.b. in the industry, but if you tell that to a prospective employer, *you* will look like the bad one.

One of the strategies of the unguided interview is to permit you to keep talking and in that way get more information from you. If your interviewer were a trained psychologist, this system might have some merit. But in the hands of amateurs, which a great many personnel people are, your ramblings may well be interpreted to your *dis*advantage.

Therefore, when you detect that the interviewer is trying to get you to talk, ask to be given some direction. Pin down the subject matter and by all means stay on the subject of the job, its requirements and your qualifications.

The Stress Interview

Another version of the unguided interview is known as the stress interview. Purposely, and with malice aforethought, it is designed to put you on the defensive. By badgering you with seemingly irrelevant questions, by pressing you to defend yourself against accusations and through the use of trick questions, the interviewer purposely attempts to rattle you.

The avowed purpose of the stress interview is to see how you react under pressure, the theory being that if you panic and lose control now, you may do the same under pressure of the job (a tenuous theory at best).

This technique can take a number of forms. You may walk into an office where two or more interviewers are in attendance, the atmosphere being more like the back room of a police station than a personnel office.

The questioner may say, "Tell us about yourself," and then not utter a word for another half hour, leaving you to fill the silence with your own voice. Another tactic of the stress interview is to ask rapid fire questions about your personal life—your finances, your spouse and family, your sex life or political opinions.

While you are trying to preserve your dignity through this inquisition, your interviewer may pick up the phone to make a personal call, leaf through a magazine, or pretend to study some papers on the desk. If you are smoking, the ashtray may be purposely hidden.

Don't fall into this trap. If the treatment gets too obnoxious, you may do one of two things: keep your cool and try to respond as calmly as possible, pointing out that you don't think the questions are relevant to the job for which you are applying, or you may become indignant, raising your voice to a low roar and telling them you wouldn't work for a company that treated applicants this way, and suggesting that they stick their job in their ears. The latter response is quite common, although it hasn't been known to result in many job offers.

Fortunately, the stress interview, which several years ago verged on becoming a national fad, has now declined in popularity. For one thing, they rarely produced usable results, since working conditions aren't usually similar to the conditions presented in a stress interview (unless the employer is the U.S. Marine Corps). For another, many corporate executives found they were losing good people because they were using this new interviewing toy.

Some Tips for the Interview

Just as no two people are exactly alike, no two interviews are conducted alike. However, some universal truths in the relationship between interviewer and applicant have evolved that apply to all interviews. The following paragraphs offer some random thoughts that may be helpful in your interview.

Show Enthusiasm. Ralph Waldo Emerson wasn't looking for a job when he said "Nothing great was ever achieved without enthusiasm," but he spoke the truth.

Enthusiasm is a great weight in the balance. When your competitor has an extra university degree and two more years of experience than you, enthusiasm can increase the odds in your favor. When asked advice by a client company who cannot decide between two equally qualified applicants, I always recommend the one who shows enthusiasm. I have yet to be proven wrong.

Even if you are not naturally outgoing and like to weigh things quietly in your mind, force yourself to show enthusiasm. If you are not sure whether you are interested in the position or the company, act as if you are. Make your interviewer believe from the beginning that you think this is a great company offering a terrific opportunity. Leave every interviewer with the best impression you can, even if you are completely disinterested in the job. Executives do not forget a good job candidate. They may be in a position to recommend you elsewhere or to another department at a later date. Experience, talent or education can get you the interview. Enthusiasm can get you the job. Use it.

Watch Your Language. Society today permits the usage of words and language that, in past generations, was considered obscene, insulting and could even get the user kicked downstairs (despite an elevator in the building). To paraphrase George Bernard Shaw, who said of the French that they didn't care what they did, as long as they pronounced it properly—today it doesn't matter what words you use, so long as you say what you mean.

An interview is no place to show off your knowledge of current vernacular. You may offend an interviewer who does not share your liberated view of expression. The use of four letter expletives in an interview may evoke a five letter word in return—l-e-a-v-e!

Interviewers are guilty of this also. Marvin B., an advertising production manager, came back from an interview that I had arranged. He related that the executive vice-president of the advertising agency, who interviewed him, hadn't used three consecutive words that were not right off the street. Perhaps the executive thought that by using that kind of language he could impress upon Marvin that he was one of the boys, and could establish a common bond with him. However, the effect on my applicant was completely the reverse. Marvin told me he couldn't work for a man who had to use that sort of language to express himself. And Marvin is far from being a Puritan. He just felt that the interview was not the place for coarse language and that however pure the intentions, it was patronizing, undignified and unnecessary. The daily conversations in some business offices would admittedly make a sailor blush, but don't speak that way on an interview.

Visual Aids. Certain occupations require visual credentials. The obvious ones are advertising, art and communications. Yet I have had people seeking jobs in these areas come to see me without portfolios, hoping to convince prospective employers that they were qualified without bringing supportive evidence.

Even if you are a beginner in any one of these areas, you should show some samples of your work. It can be school samples or unpublished material, but bring *something*. You won't get to first base without it.

Samples of your work will be helpful in occupations other than creative. Market researchers, financial analysts and salespeople are all examples. Reports, sales performance records, marketing studies, presentations—these are all evidence of your capabilities and should be shown during an interview.

No matter what your occupation, if you were given any citations, awards or letters of commendation, these documents can be the extra plus, the frosting on the cake that will have a positive effect on your interview. If you have written any articles or books which have been published, bring them along. Don't be bashful. It is permissible to blow your own horn, so long as you don't try to be the whole orchestra.

Keep Records. As soon as you can after leaving the office, write a summary of the interview. Don't wait until you get home. Your recollection may be faded by that time. The lobby, a restaurant, the subway or your car—the first place you can, write down all the names, numbers and important facts that were discussed. On page 152 you will find an example of a form that will guide you in making notes, but you can easily design one yourself.

Do not trust your memory. You may be called back for another interview days or weeks later, or asked to submit additional information about yourself. Your notes will permit you to have immediate recall when it comes to dates, names, salary information and any other data pertinent to the company and the job. You can be sure your interviewer has taken copious notes about you during and after the interview. Give yourself the same advantage.

Include in your notes any impression of the person who interviewed you, any attitudes, positive or negative, that you may have detected. It is important to note them down immediately, as impressions are fleeting. They can be very important when evaluating the interview, and can play a big part in helping you make a decision.

Record the high points of the interview. Summarize the questions and the answers you gave. These notes can save you the embarrassment of contradicting yourself in a subsequent interview.

While you are looking for a job, keep these records handy and refer to them often. Rereading them from time to time may give you new insights into your interview techniques and help improve your performance.

What Questions to Expect. There is very little any book can tell you on what to expect in an interview, except in the most general terms. However, experience has shown that there are certain questions which are asked more than others, and you should be prepared to handle them when they come.

 Questions and Answers

Here are some of the questions that occur most frequently:

(1) What have you been doing since you left your last job?
(2) What are your long-term career goals?
(3) What is your immediate objective?
(4) Why do you want to work for this company?
(5) Why did you leave your last job?

(6) What do you know about our firm?

(7) How much money do you hope to be making five years from now? Ten years from now?

(8) Are you willing to travel?

(9) Are you willing to relocate?

(10) What do you consider your greatest strength?

(11) What do you consider your greatest weakness?

(12) Do you intend to continue your education?

Answering these questions requires a careful mixture of honesty and discretion. Here are some tips on the proper answers and the reasons why.

(1) Never admit to an interviewer that you did nothing since your last job or that you went on a trip to Europe or that you took a much-needed vacation. The proper answer is, "I have been looking for the right job." If you have been unemployed for than three months, your answer may evoke a raised eyebrow from your interviewer, but it is still better than confessing that you have been resting on your laurels and your unemployment insurance.

(2) Your long-term career goal is "To achieve a high level of success in my occupation and be compensated accordingly." It is not "To go into business for myself," or "To become president of the firm," even if that is what you really want.

(3) Your immediate objective is "To become associated with a firm that will offer me the opportunity to contribute my experience and talent for the benefit of the company and my career." It is not "To make money," or "To learn as much as I can." Never give the impression that you intend to use their company as a jumping-off place for another firm.

(4) The answer to the question, "Why do you want to work for our company?" depends upon the company. If it is a well-known firm, the right answer is, "Because your firm is a leader in its field," or, "Your firm has an outstanding reputation." Don't try these answers on a small company that is not generally known to the public. It won't ring true. In this case, the reason you want to work for them is "I prefer working for a firm that I can grow with."

(5) "Why did you leave your last job?" If your previous employer has relocated, merged or gone bankrupt—then these are perfect answers. If you quit, the reason you left is, "Because I did not find the position challenging and there was no further place to go." Never say

you quit because you did not get along with your immediate supervisor or you did not agree with company policy.

If you were fired, you're in trouble no matter what the reason. There are many excuses you can give, such as, "The department was reorganized" or, "The job was eliminated." No matter how you explain it, being discharged carries a stigma. Whatever the reason for your separation, don't criticize a former employer. It sounds like sour grapes to a listener.

(6) "What do you know about our firm?" You can't bluff your way out of this one. If you really don't know anything about the company, you shouldn't be there for an interview. Your pre-interview homework should enable you to make some intelligent and factual remarks about the company, such as what it makes or the services it performs, what its annual sales volume is, how many people it employs, where its plant and offices are located, etc.

This type of information can be obtained about any firm through the use of directories and other sources described earlier. Don't repeat newspaper or trade rumors you have heard.

(7) To the question, "How much money do you hope to be making five or ten years from now," don't offer a figure. There are too many intangibles for that. The best answer is, "I hope to steadily increase my income as I make progress commensurate with the responsibility of the position." Sound trite? It is, but it's the kind of thing structured companies like to hear.

(8 and 9) Travel and relocation. If you want to work for a firm that does business nationally or internationally, you cannot categorically state that you will not travel and still survive the interview. As for relocation, you can certainly say that you would not want to relocate immediately, but you would be willing to go where the company sends you should the need arise at a later date. Don't slam the door on yourself now by adamantly refusing to consider a situation which may or may not arise in the future.

(10) What you consider your greatest strength should be related to the most important requirement of the job. If you are not strong in the major requirements of the job, you shouldn't be at the interview. If the job requires an analytical mind, then that is your greatest strength. If it is the ability to meet people, then that is your greatest strength. If you feel this is blatantly contrived, you're right. But what's the sense of answering the question if it will not help you get the job?

(11) Your greatest weakness? You can't think of any that particu-

larly stands out. You are confident that you can adjust to any situation because of your well-rounded background.

(12) On the question of continuing your education, if you do not have a degree, your answer is that you hope to be able to take evening courses to obtain your degree. If you already have one, you would be willing to continue studies that will be necessary to help you do your job better.

As we said, all interviews are different—because all interviewers are different. Therefore, no matter what preparations are made, the actual interview may offer a few surprises.

For instance, an applicant I spent two hours with, preparing him for an interview for a job as a junior financial analyst with an investment firm, reported that he was greeted by a receptionist who gave him a four-page application form to fill out. He was then ushered into an office where he was told that it was the policy of the firm to have new job applicants complete a short aptitude test.

Although thoroughly annoyed at this point, he figured that since he had invested so much time already, he would take the short test, which he found took an hour. He was then told that he would be notified by mail when to come in for a second interview. My advice to anyone presented with a similar situation would be to walk out. Any firm that considers this routine a first interview would probably be a poor place in which to work.

What Not To Do in an Interview

Don't be a comedian. Your friends may tell you that you have a great sense of humor, but save it for the next party. You may think that making jokes during an interview will lessen the tension. It may very well do that, but only for yourself. If your interviewer tells you what is supposedly a funny story—laugh, even if it hurts. But do not try to entertain in return. Be pleasant, but be serious.

Don't prejudge the company by the person who interviews you, or by the decor of the office. One applicant came back to me and said that she wouldn't work for a firm that did not care about the environment. What bothered her was a large stuffed marlin hung over the desk of the personnel manager who interviewed her. Her concern for the environment was admirable, but misplaced. The company's products had nothing to do with the environment one way or the other. The personnel officer was either a fisherman or the decoration came with the office.

Don't ask about benefits at your first interview. I have had companies tell me about job applicants whose first questions concerned the company vacation policy. Some people, just out of college and without a single day's work experience, inquire about pension and retirement plans.

You are entitled to know about a firm's benefit programs, but it's not very bright to bring it up at the first interview. When there is sufficient interest in you, they will tell you all about the benefits. Then you can make all the inquiries you want.

Don't be a name dropper. Telling your interviewer that you belong to the same country club as Jane Fergusen, the operations vice-president, or that your father was in the same fraternity with the chairman of the board, will not impress one bit. It may have the opposite effect. Your motives may be pure, but this is often perceived by the interviewer as slightly intimidating. It's like telling a cop who is giving you a ticket that you have friends at headquarters.

Don't smoke. It fouls up the air. If your interviewer is a non-smoker, it may also foul up your chances of getting the job. There is a story around personnel offices about the job applicant who chain-smoked throughout the interview, creating a blue pall over the small office. The interviewer, in a spasm of coughing and wanting to end the interview, quickly came to the final question on the checklist. "And how is your health, Miss Mullen?"

"Better than yours," she replied. "At least I don't cough all the time."

Some Things You Should Do

Do talk in terms of the needs of the company. Avoid talking about what you hope to get out of the job. To paraphrase a famous quote—ask not what your potential employer can do for you, but what you can do for the company.

Do be confident. The firm is as much in need of your services as you are in need of a job. Don't try too hard. Avoid giving the impression that you are desperate for a job, and that you will do anything to get one. Showing some independence is good. This is not easy to do when you have been out of work for a while. No one can blame you for being depressed and disillusioned when you have been pounding the sidewalk, the typewriter and your head (the latter against stone walls). Being subjected to various degrees of indifference and rejection can destroy even the strongest of egos.

You have to be a pretty good actor to hide your discouragement. It seeps through in your voice and your bearing. When things look worst, you have to look and act your best. Frank R., vice president of personnel for a major publishing company, told me that he can sense despair in an applicant through an almost imperceptible shrillness in the applicant's voice, a certain look in the eyes. It makes him uncomfortable, he said, and as a result prejudices him against the applicant.

16

After the Interview

The interview may be the high point in your job search, but it is not the last step you take. Your next act is to send a letter to your interviewer thanking her for her time. Because so few people do it, this bit of common courtesy carries power. I have seen it work.

Personnel people and department heads spend long hours interviewing all kinds of applicants. What is a special event to you is a routine chore to them. Interviewing day in and day out is tedious and repetitious. When an applicant is thoughtful enough to take the time to write a personal note, the effect is tremendous. No matter how the interview went, a well-written letter can work to your advantage.

Do not use the letter to restate your case or review the interview. It is not a sales letter. Merely express your thanks for the time and express the hope that you are being favorably considered. Mention a particular aspect of the job for which you feel especially qualified, or call attention to an important aspect of your background. Do not get maudlin. Keep it short. See the samples on pages 128 to 133.

Evaluate Your Performance

When you return home after the interview, review your performance. Try to recall what questions were asked and how you responded to them. It is painful to recall situations which you felt you handled badly, but

150

you must learn something from each interview in order to do better on the next one. Ask yourself the following questions after each interview.

* Did I forget to mention anything about my background that would have helped me?
* Did I come on too strong? Not strong enough?
* Do I have all the information I need about the job, or did I neglect to ask the right questions?
* Where did I make my biggest mistake during the interview?
* Where did I appear to get the most favorable response?
* Did I talk too much or too little?
* Did I answer all questions clearly?
* Did I make any gaffes in statements, gestures, questions or answers? Were they serious, or am I overestimating their importance?
* Did I make a good physical presentation? Was I properly dressed?

Summary of Interview

This form should be used whenever you are called in for an interview. Enter your impressions of the company, your interviewer, salary discussion—any information that will help you recall the interview. It will help you make up your mind if you are faced with more than one job offer. Make copies and use a separate form for each interview.

NAME OF FIRM: _____

ADDRESS _____ PHONE _____

PRODUCT OR SERVICE _____

POSITION _____

LOCATION _____

SALARY _____

SOURCE OF CONTACT _____
(Classified ad, direct-mail, personal, etc.)

DESCRIPTION OF POSITION _____

_____

INTERVIEWED BY _____ TITLE _____
. . . .

NOTES ON INTERVIEW _____

_____

_____

_____

_____

_____

_____

FOLLOW-UP _____

_____

_____

_____

_____

17

Finding a Job
Out of Town

How many of us have, at one time or another, entertained the idea of moving to another city?

The grass eternally seeming greener on the other side, I imagine all of us have occasionally harbored the thought of starting somewhere else. If you are like most, the greatest block to such a move is probably the question of how and where to find a job when you get there. If you are employed now, the problem becomes even greater. How do you find a job out of town when you have to report for work every day in your present job?

It's not easy, but it can be done with planning and patience. You first have to be very specific about where you want to go. Because of the special problems of long distance job-hunting, you must concentrate on one area or one city. Because it takes time to initiate and develop a campaign, you have to be sure it's the area in which you want to work.

The first step to take after you have decided where you want to work is to order a subscription to the major daily and Sunday newspaper there. You can easily find their names by consulting *Editor and Publisher*, the trade journal for the newspaper industry. This firm publishes a directory of newspapers, and is available at your library. It lists every newspaper in the country, with information about its circulation and the area it serves. Choose the paper with the largest Sunday readership. This is usually the one that carries the most help wanted classified advertising.

You can usually order a trial subscription for a short period. Read the newspaper carefully for about a month. Check the help wanted columns to see how the employment in your field shapes up. Are there jobs advertised for which you qualify? Are there enough of them to indicate an adequate market for you? Read the entire classified section, including real estate and business opportunities, as well as the rest of the newspaper. You will learn a lot about the city, its people, its business climate and its problems.

Check the Local Newspapers

A good way to get a really detailed report on a city or an area is to write to the advertising manager of the newspaper. You can find that name in the *Editor and Publisher* directory. Write that you are thinking of moving to the area and request that you be sent some demographic information. Most newspapers publish an area population analysis covering their readership. This is broken down into reader's age, income, home ownership, purchasing projections, business, employment and other statistics. These are primarily published for the information of advertisers, but a polite letter will probably get you a copy.

This type of report will reveal the complete economic make-up of an area, and with other information you can get, will help you decide if it is a viable alternative to your present environment.

Write a letter to the chamber of commerce of the city. Tell them you desire to move and to obtain a position. Mention what kind of job you are seeking and ask them to send you whatever available information that would be helpful to you. Most chambers of commerce issue material on various aspects of their localities with information on employment, housing, schools and economic make-up.

Write to the state chapter of the National Association of Personnel Consultants (addresses can be found on page 173) and request a list of employment agencies in the locality.

After all this, if you decide that the area looks good to you, use the newspapers to reply to help wanted ads that seem to fit your situation. Send in your resume, and be sure to attach a covering letter explaining your objectives, salary history and any other information that may be helpful.

Keep in mind, however, that salary levels in various cities can vary and what is average in one can be way out of line in another. The U.S. Department of Labor issues a number of salary-and-wage level publications covering different areas in the country. It is always useful to write to the State Labor Department and to a regional or city commerce and industry association to get the local wage levels for your job.

If your present or recent salary tends to price you out of that market, deal with the point directly in your covering letter by saying that you are primarily interested in moving to that section or city and that your salary requirements would be the prevailing local standard.

Firms in smaller cities sometimes have difficulty obtaining qualified executives, and would probably welcome applicants from other areas. Indicate in your covering letter that you would be willing to come out and see them for an exploratory interview. Do *not* mention reimbursement for travel or relocation expenses. If interested in you, the company will probably bring up the subject in its reply.

Also send your letter and resume to employment agencies. They are good sources, as they usually are on top of the local job market.

Make full use of the direct-mail method of job-hunting. With careful use of directories, you can pinpoint the firms located in your chosen area and direct your applications to the proper individuals.

Study the trade journals serving your field. Their help wanted ads may offer possibilities in the area you are seeking. It would also be a good idea to do a little self-advertising in these journals, indicating your choice of location.

Visit the Area

Your biggest task will be taking the time to go out to the area and look it over. You may have to use your vacation or take time off. Plan to spend at least a week. Visit the employment agencies. Make a personal call on the local chamber of commerce. Try to arrange interviews in advance.

It is a good idea to take your spouse along. After all, that person has to like where you are going to work and will have to live there too.

Unless you have a lot of money in the bank, don't make a move without either having a job or pretty good evidence that there are possibilities for someone with your background. This is particularly true if you are leaving a metropolitan area for a smaller city where the jobs are scarcer.

One thing you must have is a pioneer spirit. If you have been settled in your present city and your present job for some time, you will be taking a calculated risk. But without risks, there are no rewards. Don't rush your decision. Study the pros and cons carefully, and if the signs are encouraging—go. The longer you wait, the harder it will become.

18

The Mature Job Hunter

If you are forty or over, you will probably discover that the road to new employment gets steeper with every additional year. However, despite the barriers designed to keep you on the fringe of the job market, you *can* get a job—you can get a good job—but your campaign has to be carefully planned and unflaggingly executed. You will need job-hunting skills, which this book can help you with, and patience, which you have to acquire by yourself. Patience is the vital ingredient.

We all know that the usual prejudices against over-forty job candidates are pure bunk. We also all know that the law books are full of statutes barring discrimination. The problem is that the prejudices are commonly held (even defensively by many employers) and while there are very few outrightly provable age-discrimination cases, it does indeed exist.

What are some of the reasons that employers take a dim view of over-forty? Well, they say supervisors often feel uncomfortable with subordinates older than themselves. And they add, managers like to be surrounded by younger people; executives fear those with more experience than themselves who are in lower job categories; anyone over forty and looking for a job is automatically a loser; older people find it hard to accept criticism and are too set in their ways; finally, people over forty have a higher share of health-related problems and are riskier for the company.

It is easy to see when these things are listed on paper how absurd they are, and in fact the same criticisms can be applied to anyone of any age in an employer-employee relationship. But absurdity doesn't play a role in prejudice, and as silly as these notions are, they are widely held by a great many employers and effectively reinforced by personnel departments in large corporations (which are largely staffed, in practice, by young people). Therefore, the over-forty individual has to shape his or her strategy to meet the situation.

Plan Carefully

The first and most important consideration is that if you have a job, don't—under any circumstances—leave until you have a firm offer from another company. The over-forty bias doesn't seem to come into play if you are being hired away from another firm.

The second consideration is that every method of job-hunting we talked about must be followed through with extreme care. *All* the lines must be working simultaneously. Don't skip any of the methods outlined.

The third consideration is to prepare your resume with extreme care, using the functional form. Keep reworking it until it is the kind of resume that you would be interested in if you were doing the hiring.

The next tactic is to utilize organizations that are specifically designed to meet the needs of over-forty job hunters. There are a number of these, and you can usually get their names through your local chamber of commerce, public library advisory service, public service groups and in many cases, religious organizations. The best known, of course, are the Forty Plus clubs, originally organized in Boston in 1939 and now, on a loosely coordinated association basis, are located in many parts of the country and in most major cities.

Through their many years of experience, the Forty Plus clubs have tailored programs to both the psychological and practical needs of the over-forty job hunter. They can be fairly effective in helping you get placed. Because many members are former executives of major companies, they often have entree to and information about firms which is hard for an outsider to come by.

Since the clubs are only loosely connected, requirements for membership vary. One advantage, though, is that a member in good standing who moves to another area can transfer the membership without any problem.

While these clubs are useful for the over-forty job seeker, it must be kept in mind that they *are* clubs. The New York club, for example, requires that prospective members, in addition to being over forty, be

U.S. citizens, have earned over $20,000 a year, must submit six business references, and go through a screening process. In addition, there is an entrance fee. However, once in, a member can expect substantial help in resume preparation, personal and skills evaluation, referral services and general support in job hunting. For many, these clubs have been the key to new and better jobs when the job market seemed almost closed.

The best bet for an over-forty seeker on the usual job hunt is to use personal contacts and a carefully prepared resume. While employment agencies are sometimes useful, they are generally marginal in producing job offers for the older worker. Even if they don't share the usual age prejudices they are frequently in the position of having to carry out a prospective employer's wishes, whether they acknowledge those wishes or not.

Trade associations and the classified ads in trade magazines are also strong bets for those over forty. All in all, the direct mail method is the best and should be used to its fullest. Nevertheless, it is essential that you do not overlook *any* of the methods. The one that might be statistically marginal for everyone else is the one that just might get you the job.

One last note. While executive recruiters are always on the prowl for good material, be extremely wary of any that entice you in and then offer you their services for a fee. They are often aimed at your wallet instead of your career. Good recruiters are well paid by their corporate clients and their primary interest is in getting the right person into the job slot. If they want fees from their candidates, then they probably aren't getting fees from their corporations. Steer clear. If in doubt, check the firm out with a local Better Business Bureau and local licensing authorities.

19

How to
Use Your Time Wisely

A book on successful job hunting would not be complete without a few words about the proper utilization of your most important asset—time.

If you are unemployed, time can turn into your worst enemy, if you let it. The choice is yours. On the other hand, establishing a few simple rules and applying some self-discipline can make your time pay off.

The first rule of efficient time use is: start now. Not tomorrow or Monday morning or after lunch, but right this minute N-O-W! This is especially true for job hunting. It is too easy to find reasons to put off the actual start. Here are some of the more common ones: "I can't look for a job until the Sunday papers come out"; "Business is slow in the summer. I'll start looking in the fall"; "I'll start after the holidays" (there are always holidays); "I still have ten weeks to go on my unemployment insurance"; "There's no rush, I can get a job anytime I want."

Don't let yourself fall into these traps of self-deception. Unless you are very lucky, days, weeks and months fly by very quickly. The sooner you get started, the sooner you will reach your goal of getting the job you want. How can you avoid squandering precious time? Here are a few common-sense steps.

(1) *Establish quotas.* This is a very effective way to use time efficiently. For instance, when performing each activity in your job-hunting

159

campaign, set goals. Don't aim so high that you cannot accomplish what you set out to do, but make your quota high enough to keep yourself busy and your campaign moving steadily ahead. Don't just think about your goals. Write them down on a piece of paper and stick to them.

For example, you are answering classified advertising in the paper daily. Set a quota of answering ten ads a week. In your direct mail campaign, set a quota of three letters a day.

By setting quotas and meeting them, you guarantee that a sufficient number of letters and resumes will go out each day and each week. The cumulative effect will pleasantly surprise you. Schedule yourself to maintain contact with each employment agency you choose once a week and stick to it. Don't worry about bothering them—that's what they're in business for.

(2) *Make* Things To Be Done Today *lists*. Every morning, or the night before, write down everything you have to do for the day ahead, no matter how trivial, so long as it pertains to your job hunt. And try to get everything done that day, no matter how long it takes. Whatever you can't accomplish and is left over, put at the head of tomorrow's list. But make the lists reasonable. Long lists are rarely completed, and the discouragement is cumulative.

(3) *Keep regular hours*. Looking for a job should be considered a full-time job in itself. This means you should set regular hours for yourself. Not having an office to go to every morning easily leads to late rising, leisurely breakfasts and a vacation-like daily routine. In this way, the days and weeks go by very quickly, with very little to show for them.

Set your clock so you get up early enough to be actively working on your campaign by 9:00 AM—whether it's writing a letter or a resume or calling on a company or agency. Use the early morning time to make up your *To Do* list. Don't quit early in the afternoon because you think you have nothing to do. Go to the library and study a few trade journals. Drop into an employment agency you haven't covered. Commandeer the nearest telephone booth and call some new contacts or renew some old ones.

The nine to five routine accomplishes two important things. There is less time for idleness and self-pity, and since it is a forced regimen, it makes you more productive in your job hunt. If you have a family at home, everyone is better off, psychologically, when you maintain a daily routine.

We all have 168 hours in a week, not one second more or less. It's what you do with them that distinguishes your accomplishments from everyone else's. Let these 168 hours slip away in activities like watching TV or wandering aimlessly around the house wondering why things aren't working out, and you won't accomplish the things you want to do. Control those 168 hours by using each one productively and your goals will be realized.

Appendix 1

Test Your Success Qualities

On the following chart, check the boxes which you believe represent your strengths in each of the qualities listed. They are all positive attributes that would contribute to success in any career.

If you have been completely honest with yourself, a quick analysis of the completed chart will give you a general idea of your strengths and weaknesses.

	Extremely	Very	Moderately	Not very	Not at all
AGGRESSIVE					
ASSERTIVE					
CALM					
CHEERFUL					
COMPETITIVE					
CONFIDENT					
COURTEOUS					
CREATIVE					
COOPERATIVE					
DEPENDABLE					
EFFICIENT					
ENERGETIC					
ENTHUSIASTIC					
FIRM					
FORCEFUL					
FRIENDLY					
IMAGINATIVE					
INTELLIGENT					
LOGICAL					
OPTIMISTIC					
ORGANIZED					
OUTGOING					
PERSEVERING					
POISED					
PRECISE					

	Extremely	Very	Moderately	Not very	Not at all
REASONABLE					
SELF-ASSURED					
SELF-CONTROLLED					
SINCERE					
STABLE					
STEADY					
STRONG-MINDED					
TACTFUL					
THOROUGH					
TOLERANT					
TOUGH					
TRUSTWORTHY					
UNASSUMING					
UNDERSTANDING					
CONSIDERATE					

Appendix 2

Information Sources by Occupation

ACCOUNTING

Organizations
American Institute of CPAs
666 Fifth Avenue
New York, NY 10019

National Association of
    Accountants
919 Third Avenue
New York, NY 10022

National Society of Public
    Accountants
1717 Pennsylvania Avenue
Washington, DC 20006

Publications
CPA JOURNAL
355 Lexington Avenue
New York, NY 10017

JOURNAL OF ACCOUNTANCY
1211 Avenue of the Americas
New York, NY 10036

ADMINISTRATION

Organizations
Administrative Management
    Society
Willow Grove, PA 19090

American Institute of Management
125 East 38th Street
New York, NY 10016

American Management Association
135 West 50th Street
New York, NY 10020

Publications
ADVANCED MANAGEMENT
    JOURNAL
135 West 50th Street
New York, NY 10020

CONFERENCE BOARD
    RECORD
845 Third Avenue
New York, NY 10022

MANAGEMENT REVIEW
135 West 50th Street
New York, NY 10020

MANAGEMENT WORLD
Maryland Road
Willow Grove, PA 19090

SUPERVISORY MANAGE-
    MENT
135 West 50th Street
New York, NY 10020

POOR'S REGISTER OF COR-
PORATION, DIRECTORS
AND EXECUTIVES
345 Hudson Street
New York, NY 10014

ADVERTISING

Organizations
Advertising Council
825 Third Avenue
New York, NY 10022

Advertising Research Foundation
3 East 54th Street
New York, NY 10022

Association of National Advertisers
155 East 44th Street
New York, NY 10017

Direct Mail/Marketing Association
230 Park Avenue
New York, NY 10017

Publications
ADVERTISING AGE
740 Rush Street
Chicago, IL 60611

ADVERTISING NEWS OF
NEW YORK
230 Park Avenue
New York, NY 10017

DIRECT MARKETING
MAGAZINE
224 Seventh Avenue
Garden City, NY 11530

MADISON AVENUE
HANDBOOK
17 East 48th Street
New York, NY 10017

STANDARD RATE & DATA
SERVICE
5201 Old Orchard Road
Skokie, IL 60076
(Publishers of general information
for advertising agencies and
advertisers. Separate
directories for: Consumer

magazines, business magazines,
newspapers, radio and TV
stations, farm publications
and other specialized media)

ADVERTISING AGENCIES

Organizations
American Association of
Advertising Agencies
200 Park Avenue
New York, NY 10017

Western States Advertising
Association
5900 Wilshire Boulevard
Los Angeles, CA 90036

Publications
ADVERTISING NEWS
NEW YORK
230 Park Avenue
New York, NY 10017

AAAA ROSTER
American Association of
Advertising Agencies
200 Park Avenue
New York, NY 10017

MADISON AVENUE
HANDBOOK
444 East 52nd Street
New York, NY 10022

STANDARD DIRECTORY OF
ADVERTISING AGENCIES
5201 Old Orchard Road
Skokie, IL 60076

ARCHITECTURE

Organizations
American Institute of Architects
1735 New York Avenue, N.W.
Washington, DC 20006

Society of American Registered
Architects
600 South Michigan Avenue
Chicago, IL 60601

Publications
AMERICAN INSTITUTE OF
    ARCHITECTS JOURNAL
1735 New York Avenue
Washington, DC 20006

ARCHITECTURAL FORUM
130 East 59th Street
New York, NY 10022

ARCHITECTURAL RECORD
1221 Avenue of Americas
New York, NY 10020

PROGRESSIVE
    ARCHITECTURE
600 Summer Street
Stamford, CT 06904

BANKING

Organizations
American Bankers Association
1120 Connecticut Avenue, NW
Washington, DC 20036

American Institute of Banking
1120 Connecticut Avenue, NW
Washington, DC 20036

National Association of Mutual
    Savings Banks
200 Park Avenue
New York, NY 10017

Publications
AMERICAN BANKER
525 West 42nd Street
New York, NY 10036

BANKING MAGAZINE
350 Broadway
New York, NY 10013

JOURNAL OF COMMERCIAL
    BANK LENDING
Philadelphia National Bank
    Building
Philadelphia, PA 19107

SAVINGS BANK JOURNAL
200 Park Avenue
New York, NY 10017

AMERICAN BANK
    DIRECTORY
Warren Drive
Norcross, GA 30093

BOOK PUBLISHING

Organizations
Association of American Publishers
1 Park Avenue
New York, NY 10016

Publications
BOOK PRODUCTION
    INDUSTRY
Box 415
Berea, OH 44017

PUBLISHERS WEEKLY
1180 Avenue of the Americas
New York, NY 10036

LITERARY MARKET PLACE
1180 Avenue of the Americas
New York, NY 10036

CHEMICAL ENGINEERING

Organizations
American Chemical Society
1155 16th Street, N.W.
Washington, DC 20036

American Institute of Chemical
    Engineers
345 East 47th Street
New York, NY 10017

Publications
CHEMICAL ENGINEERING
1221 Avenue of the Americas
New York, NY 10020

CHEMICAL ENGINEERING
    CATALOG
600 Summer Street
Stamford, CT 06904

COMMERCIAL ART

Organizations
Art Director's Club
488 Madison Avenue
New York, NY 10022

Publications
ART DIRECTION
19 West 44th Street
New York, NY 10036

GRAPHICS, USA
535 Fifth Avenue
New York, NY 10017

ARTS & CRAFTS MARKET
9933 Alliance Road
Cincinnati, OH 45242

CREDIT

Organizations
International Credit Association
375 Jackson Avenue
St. Louis, MO 63130

National Association of Credit
    Management
475 Park Avenue South
New York, NY 10016

National Institute of Credit
3000 Marcus Avenue
Lake Success, NY 11040

Publications
CREDIT & FINANCIAL
    MANAGEMENT
475 Park Avenue South
New York, NY 10016

CREDIT WORLD
375 Jackson Avenue
St. Louis, MO 63130

NATIONAL DIRECTORY OF
    FINANCE COMPANIES
714 Neosho Boulevard
Neosho, MO 64850

COMPUTERS

Organizations
American Federation of
    Information Processing
    Societies
210 Summit Avenue
Montvale, NJ 07645

Association for Computing
    Machinery
1133 Avenue of the Americas
New York, NY 10036

Association of Data Processing
    Service Organizations
210 Summit Avenue
Montvale, NJ 07645

Data Processing Management
    Association
505 Busse Highway
Park Ridge, IL 60068

Publications
ADP NEWSLETTER
430 Park Avenue
New York, NY 10022

COMPUTERS &
    MANAGEMENT
Fairview Park
Elmsford, NY 10523

WHO IS RELATED TO WHOM
    IN THE COMPUTER
    INDUSTRY
Fairview Park
Elmsford, NY 10523

WORLD WIDE DIRECTORY OF
    COMPUTER COMPANIES
200 East Ohio Street
New York, NY 60611

ECONOMICS

Organizations
National Association of Business
    Economics
28349 Chagrin Boulevard
Cleveland, OH 44122

Publications
QUARTERLY JOURNAL OF
    ECONOMICS
605 Third Avenue
New York, NY 10016

AMERICAN ECONOMIC
   ASSOCIATION
   DIRECTORY
1313 21st Street South
Nashville, TN 37212

ELECTRONICS

Organizations
Electronic Industries Association
2001 Eye Street
Washington, DC 20006

Publications
ELECTRONIC BUSINESS
221 Columbus Avenue
Boston, MA 02116

ELECTRONIC DESIGN
50 Essex Street
Rochelle Park, NJ 07662

ELECTRONICS PRODUCTS
   MAGAZINE
645 Stewart Avenue
Garden City, NY 11530

ELECTRONICS
1221 Avenue of the Americas
New York, NY 10020

FINANCE

Organizations
Financial Executives Institute
633 Third Avenue
New York, NY 10017

Publications
BARRON's NATIONAL
   BUSINESS & FINANCIAL
   WEEKLY
22 Cortlandt Street
New York, NY 10004

FINANCIAL EXECUTIVE
633 Third Avenue
New York, NY 10017

FINANCIAL WORLD
919 Third Avenue
New York, NY 10022

MONEY MANAGER
1 State Street Plaza
New York, NY 10007

HOME ECONOMICS

Organizations
American Home Economics
   Association
2010 Massachusetts Avenue, N.W.
Washington, DC 20036

Publications
FORECAST FOR HOME
   ECONOMICS
50 West 44th Street
New York, NY 10036

JOURNAL OF HOME
   ECONOMICS
2010 Massachusetts Avenue,.NW
Washington, DC 20036

WHAT'S NEW IN HOME
   ECONOMICS
401 North Broad Street
Philadelphia, PA 19108

AHEA DIRECTORY
2010 Massachusetts Avenue, NW
Washington, DC 20036

HOSPITAL

Organizations
American Hospital Association
840 North Lake Shore Drive
Chicago, IL 60611

Publications
HOSPITAL FINANCIAL
   MANAGEMENT
840 North Lake Shore Drive
Chicago, IL 60611

HOSPITAL TOPICS
734 Sesta Key Circle
Sarasota, FL 33581

GUIDE TO HEALTH CARE
   FIELD
840 North Lake Shore Drive
Chicago, IL 60611

HOTEL AND MOTEL

Organizations
American Hotel & Motel
   Association
888 Seventh Avenue
New York, NY 10019

Publications
GENEVA NEWSLETTER
   MANAGEMENT
121 West 45th Street
New York, NY 10036

HOTEL & MOTEL
845 Chicago Avenue
Evanston, IL 60202

HOTEL & MOTEL RED BOOK
888 Seventh Avenue
New York, NY 10019

INTERNATIONAL HOTEL
   DIRECTORY
1418 South Andrews Avenue
Ft. Lauderdale, FL 33311

INDUSTRIAL DESIGN

Organizations
Industrial Designers Society of
   America
1750 Old Meadow Road
McLean, VA 22101

Publications
DESIGN NEWS
221 Columbus Avenue
Boston, MA 01772

INDUSTRIAL DESIGN
1515 Broadway
New York, NY 10036

INDUSTRIAL DESIGNERS
   SOCIETY OF AMERICA
   JOURNAL
Fairview Park
Elmsford, NY 10523

MACHINE DESIGN
111 Chester Avenue
Cleveland, OH 44114

INSURANCE

Organizations
National Association of
   Independent Insurers
2600 River Road
Des Plaines, IL 60018

National Insurers Association
2400 South Michigan Avenue
Chicago, IL 60616

Insurance Information Institute
110 William Street
New York, NY 10038

Publications
BEST'S WEEKLY NEWS
   DIGEST
Oldwick, NJ 08858

INSURANCE ADVOCATE
45 John Street
New York, NY 10038

INSURANCE WEEK
2322 National Bank Building
Seattle, WA 98154

JOURNALISM

Organizations
American Society of Newspaper
   Editors
Box 551
Easton, PA 18042

Associated Press Managing
   Editors
50 Rockefeller Plaza
New York, NY 10020

International Association of
   Business Communicators
870 Market Street
San Francisco, CA 94102

Publications
PROGRAMS IN JOURNALISM
(List of Journalism Schools)
Missouri School of Journalism
Columbia, MO 65201

THE QUILL
35 East Wacker Drive
Chicago, IL 60601

FOLIO
125 Elm Street
New Canaan, CT 06840

EDITOR & PUBLISHER
(Market Guide)
(Syndicate Directory)
575 Lexington Avenue
New York, NY 10022

LIBRARY

Organizations
American Library Association
50 East Huron Street
Chicago, IL 60611

Special Libraries Association
235 Park Avenue South
New York, NY 10018

Publications
AMERICAN LIBRARIES
50 East Huron Street
Chicago, IL 60611

LIBRARY JOURNAL
1180 Avenue of the Americas
New York, NY 10036

WILSON LIBRARY BULLETIN
950 University Avenue
Bronx, NY 10452

ALA MEMBERSHIP
    DIRECTORY
50 East Huron Street
Chicago, IL 60611

MARKETING/
MARKET RESEARCH

Organizations
American Marketing Association
222 South Riverside Plaza
Chicago, IL

Market Research Association
P.O. Box 1415
Grand Central Station
New York, NY 10017

Publications
JOURNAL OF MARKETING
    RESEARCH
222 South Riverside Plaza
Chicago, IL 60606

MARKETING &
    COMMUNICATIONS
475 Park Avenue South
New York, NY 10016

ADVERTISING AGE
740 Rush Street
Chicago, IL 60611

INDUSTRIAL MARKETING
740 Rush Street
Chicago, IL 60611

PERSONNEL

Organizations
American Management Association
135 West 50th Street
New York, NY 10020

American Society for Personnel
    Administration
30 Park Drive
Berea, OH 44107

Publications
PERSONNEL
    ADMINISTRATOR
30 Park Drive
Berea, OH 44107

PERSONNEL JOURNAL
866 West 18th Street
Costa Mesa, CA 92627

PERSONNEL
135 West 50th Street
New York, NY 10020

PENSION WORLD
6285 Barfield
Atlanta, GA 30328

PHOTOGRAPHY

Organizations
Photographic Society of America
2005 Walnut Street
Philadelphia, PA 19103

Publications
INDUSTRIAL PHOTOGRAPHY
475 Park Avenue South
New York, NY 10016

PHOTOGRAPHIC TRADE
    NEWS
250 Fulton Avenue
Hempstead, NY 11550

PHOTOGRAPHY MARKET
    PLACE
Box 1807
Ann Arbor, MI 48106

PRINTING & GRAPHIC ARTS

Organizations
American Institute of Graphic Arts
1059 Third Avenue
New York, NY 10022

Printing Industries of America
1730 Lynn Street
Arlington, VA 22209

Publications
GRAPHIC ARTS MONTHLY
666 Fifth Avenue
New York, NY 10019

PRINTING TRADES BLUE
    BOOK
79 Madison Avenue
New York, NY 10003

PRINTING IMPRESSIONS
401 North Broad Street
Philadelphia, PA 19108

PUBLISHING—MAGAZINES

Organizations
American Business Press, Inc.
205 East 42nd Street
New York, NY 10017

American Society of Magazine
    Editors
575 Lexington Avenue
New York, NY 10022

American Society of Business
    Press Editors
221 North LaSalle Street
Chicago, IL 60601

Publications
FOLIO: THE MAGAZINE FOR
    MAGAZINE
    MANAGEMENT
125 Elm Street
New Canaan, CT 06840

STANDARD RATE & DATA
    SERVICE
Skokie, IL 60076
(Complete list of consumer and
    trade magazines with data on
    circulation, personnel,
    advertising rates, format and
    mechanical reproduction.)

RETAIL

Organizations
National Retail Merchants
    Association
100 West 31st Street
New York, NY 10001

Publications
CHAIN STORE EXECUTIVE
425 Park Avenue
New York, NY 10022

STORES MAGAZINE
100 West 31st Street
New York, NY 10001

CHAIN STORE AGE
425 Park Avenue
New York, NY 10022

DIRECTORY OF
    SUPERMARKET,
    GROCERY AND
    CONVENIENCE CHAINS
425 Park Avenue
New York, NY 10022

TELEVISION

Organizations
National Academy of Television
    Arts & Sciences
291 La Cienega Boulevard
Beverly Hills, CA 90211

National Association of
    Broadcasters
1771 North Street, N.W.
Washington, DC 20036

Television Bureau of Advertising
1345 Avenue of the Americas
New York, NY 10020

Publications
BROADCASTING
1735 DeSales Street, N.W.
Washington, DC 20036

EDUCATIONAL &
    INDUSTRIAL TELEVISION
51 Sugar Hollow Road
Danbury, CT 06810

RADIO & TELEVISION
    WEEKLY
254 East 31st Street
New York, NY 10001

PUBLIC RELATIONS

Organizations
Public Relations Society of
    America
845 Third Avenue
New York, NY 10022

Publications
O'DWYER'S DIRECTORY OF
    PUBLIC RELATIONS
    FIRMS
271 Madison Avenue
New York, NY 10016

PUBLIC RELATIONS
    REGISTER
845 Third Avenue
New York, NY 10022

TRAVEL & TOURISM

Organizations
American Society of Travel
    Agents (ASTA)
711 Fifth Avenue
New York, NY 10022

Publications
ASTA TRAVEL NEWS
488 Madison Avenue
New York, NY 10022

TRAVEL AGENT MAGAZINE
2 West 46th Street
New York, NY 10036

TRAVEL TRADE MAGAZINE
605 Fifth Avenue
New York, NY 10017

TRAVEL WEEKLY
1 Park Avenue
New York, NY 10016

Appendix 3

Members of the National Association
of Personnel Consultants
(Employment Agency State Associations)

ALABAMA EMPLOYMENT
   ASSOCIATION
George Barnes
Snelling and Snelling
1217 North Memorial Parkway
Huntsville, AL 35801

ARIZONA ASSOCIATION OF
   PERSONNEL
   CONSULTANTS
Ira Marks
Fortune of Phoenix
4001 N. 32nd Street
Phoenix, AZ 85018

ARKANSAS PRIVATE
   EMPLOYMENT AGENCY
   ASSOCIATION
Ed Schulte
Dunhill of Little Rock, AR
608 University Tower Building
Little Rock, AR 72204

CALIFORNIA EMPLOYMENT
   ASSOCIATION
Robert Read
Sales Consultants
50 California Street, 35th Floor
San Francisco, CA 94111

COLORADO ASSOCIATION OF
   PERSONNEL SERVICES
Craig Fetterolf
Phillips Personnel

828 17th Street, #814
Denver, CO 80202

CONNECTICUT CHAPTER/
   NATIONAL ASSOCIATION
   OF PERSONNEL
   CONSULTANTS
Louis M. Hipp, III
Hipp-Waters Associates
64 Greenwich Avenue
Greenwich, CT 06830

CAPITAL AREA PERSONNEL
   SERVICES ASSOCIATION
J. D. Maynard
National Resources, Inc.
1700 East Gude Drive
Rockville, MD 20850

PERSONNEL SERVICES
   ASSOCIATION OF
   DELAWARE
Barry S. Schlecker
Barry Personnel
901 Washington Street
Wilmington, DE 19801

FLORIDA ASSOCIATION OF
   PERSONNEL
   CONSULTANTS
Norman Floyd
Snelling and Snelling
1135 NW 23rd Avenue
Gainesville, FL 32601

GEORGIA ASSOCIATION OF
PERSONNEL
CONSULTANTS
Betty Arnold
Arnold Personnel Services, Inc.
1945 The Exchange, #310
Atlanta, GA 30339

HAWAII ASSOCIATION OF
PERSONNEL
CONSULTANTS
Harold Yokoyama
Associated Services Limited
1164 Bishop Street
Honolulu, HI 96813

ILLINOIS ASSOCIATION OF
PERSONNEL
CONSULTANTS
Hellen Dawson
Professional Employment, Inc.
5005 Newport Drive, #104
Rolling Meadows, IL 60008

ASSOCIATED EMPLOYMENT
AGENCIES OF INDIANA
Mr. L. Deane Shepard
Century Personnel
3737 North Meridan Street
Indianapolis, IN 46208

IOWA ASSOCIATION OF
PERSONNEL
CONSULTANTS
Philip M. Huber
Gateway Careers
307 Tucker Bldg.
Clinton, IA 52732

KENTUCKY ASSOCIATION OF
PRIVATE EMPLOYMENT
SERVICES
Rachael Nelson
Employer's Personnel, Inc.
4010 Dupont Circle
Louisville, KY 40207

LOUISIANA ASSOCIATION OF
PERSONNEL
CONSULTANTS
Rodney Driggers
Driggers & Blackwell Personnel
320 Neal Street
Ruston, LA 71270

MASSACHUSETTS CHAPTER/
NATIONAL ASSOCIATION
OF PERSONNEL
CONSULTANTS
Bernard Hirsch
Quality Personnel
339 Hancock
N. Quincy, MA 02171

MICHIGAN ASSOCIATION OF
PERSONNEL
CONSULTANTS
William J. Tripp
Management Recruiters of
Dearborn
1 Parklane Boulevard
Dearborn, MI 48126

MINNESOTA ASSOCIATION OF
PERSONNEL
CONSULTANTS
Ceil Kelly
Business Personnel, Inc.
2345 Rice Street, Suite 228
Roseville, MN 55113

MISSISSIPPI ASSOCIATION OF
PERSONNEL
CONSULTANTS
Jim Tatum
Tatum Personnel Service, Inc.
POB 12483
Jackson, MS 39211

MISSOURI ASSOCIATION OF
PERSONNEL
CONSULTANTS
Allen M. Oldfield
Professional Career Development
7777 Bonhomme, Suite 1326
Clayton, MO 63105

NEBRASKA PLACEMENT
SERVICE ASSOCIATION
Chuck Schramm
AA Personnel Lincoln, Inc.
5620 "N" Street
Lincoln, NE 68510

NEW HAMPSHIRE PRIVATE
EMPLOYMENT
ASSOCIATION

David J. Craig
Craig's Criterion, Inc.
160 South River Road
Bedford, NH 03102

NEW JERSEY ASSOCIATION
OF PERSONNEL
CONSULTANTS
Frank Sgambati
Kenwood Associates, Inc.
30 Galesi Drive
Wayne, NJ 07470

ASSOCIATION OF PERSONNEL
CONSULTANTS OF
NEW YORK
Carl F. Denny
Carlden Personnel Services
10740 Queens Boulevard
New York, NY 11372

NORTH CAROLINA
ASSOCIATION OF
PERSONNEL
CONSULTANTS
Jerry Cline
Personnel Specialists
P.O. Box 30294
Raleigh, NC 27622

OHIO ASSOCIATION OF
PERSONNEL
CONSULTANTS
Jack Richardson
Opportunity Consultants, Inc.
432 Walnut Street, Suite 208
Cincinnati, OH 45202

OKLAHOMA ASSOCIATION OF
PRIVATE EMPLOYMENT
SERVICE
Margaret Wick
Wick Personnel
7030 South Yale, #410
Tulsa, OK 74177

OREGON ASSOCIATION OF
PERSONNEL
CONSULTANTS
Gary Pagenstecher
Pagenstecher's Placement Agency
715 S.W. Morrison Street
Portland, OR 97205

PENNSYLVANIA
ASSOCIATION OF
PERSONNEL
CONSULTANTS
David Teeple
Action Personnel-Jenkintown
27 Fox Pavilion
Jenkintown, PA 19046

RHODE ISLAND CHAPTER/
NATIONAL ASSOCIATION
OF PERSONNEL
CONSULTANTS
Mary Shaw
New England Consultants, Inc.
Howard Building
10 Dorrance Street
Providence, RI 02903

SOUTH CAROLINA
ASSOCIATION OF
PERSONNEL SERVICES
Ted F. McCulloch
Beall Associates
P.O. Box 5042
Spartanburg, SC 29304

TENNESSEE ASSOCIATION OF
PERSONNEL
CONSULTANTS
W. Jerry Tillman
Dunhill Personnel
1 Airways Plaza, #514
1283 Murfreesboro Road
Nashville, TN 37217

TEXAS ASSOCIATION OF
PERSONNEL
CONSULTANTS
Beverly Scott
Career Woman Personnel
Consultants
1525 Elm Street
Dallas, TX 75201

UTAH ASSOCIATION OF
EMPLOYMENT AGENCIES
Dave Goodwill
Creative Employment Service
336 South 300 East
Salt Lake City, UT 84111

VIRGINIA ASSOCIATION OF
PERSONNEL SERVICES
Harry D. Jarvis
Management Consultants, Ltd.
18 Kroger Executive Center
Norfolk, VA 23502

WASHINGTON ASSOCIATION
OF PERSONNEL SERVICES
Evan McCord
Overlake Employment Service
11101 N.E. 8th
Bellevue, WA 98004

WEST VIRGINIA PRIVATE
EMPLOYMENT SERVICE
ASSOCIATION
James P. West
Snelling and Snelling
1007½ Market Plaza
Wheeling, WV 26003

WISCONSIN ASSOCIATION OF
PERSONNEL
CONSULTANTS
Robert Richmond
Professional Recruiters
200 Executive Drive
Brookfield, WI 53005

Appendix 4

Other Useful Directories

COLLEGE PLACEMENT
  ANNUAL
P.O. Box 2263
Bethlehem, PA 18001

ENCYCLOPEDIA OF
  ASSOCIATIONS
Gale Research Company
Book Tower Building
Detroit, MI 48226

FORTUNE DOUBLE 500
  DIRECTORY
Fortune Magazine
Rockefeller Center
New York, NY 10020

DIRECTORY OF COLLEGE
  RECRUITING
  PERSONNEL
College Placement Council
P.O. Box 2263
Bethlehem, PA 18001

GUIDE TO AMERICAN
  DIRECTORIES
B. Klein, Inc.
11 Third Street
Rye, NY 10580

JOB FACT SHEET LIST
Council for Career Planning
310 Madison Avenue
New York, NY 10022

MILLION DOLLAR
  DIRECTORY
Dun & Bradstreet Co.
99 Church Street
New York, NY 10007

DIRECTORY OF RESOURCES
  FOR AFFIRMATIVE
  RECRUITMENT
Equal Employment Opportunity
  Commission
2401 E Street, N.W.
Washington, DC 20506

MOODY's INDUSTRIAL
  MANUAL
99 Church Street
New York, NY 10007

POOR's REGISTER OF
  CORPORATIONS,
  DIRECTORS AND
  EXECUTIVES
345 Hudson Street
New York, NY 10014

STANDARD DIRECTORY OF
  ADVERTISERS
National Register Publishing Co.
5201 Old Orchard Road
Skokie, IL 60076

SOURCES OF STATE
 INFORMATION & STATE
 INDUSTRIAL
 DIRECTORIES
State Chamber of Commerce Dept.
Chamber of Commerce of the U.S.
1615 H. Street, N.W.
Washington, DC 20006

THOMAS REGISTER OF
 AMERICAN
 MANUFACTURERS
1 Penn Plaza
New York, NY 10001

U.S. INDUSTRIAL DIRECTORY
1200 Summer Street
Stamford, CT 06905

WHO'S WHO IN FINANCE &
 INDUSTRY
200 East Ohio Street
Chicago, IL 60611

DIRECTORY OF JOB HUNTING
 CONTACTS
Performance Dynamics
400 Lanidex Plaza
Parsippany, NJ

NATIONAL DIRECTORY OF
 WOMEN'S EMPLOYMENT
 ORGANIZATIONS
Wider Opportunities for Women
1649 K Street, N.W.
Washington, DC 20006

Bibliography

Albee, Lou, *Job Hunting After Forty*. New York, N.Y.: Arc Books.

Barnewall, Gordon, *Succeed As A Job Applicant*. New York, N.Y.: Arco Publishing, Inc.

Boll, Carl R., *Executive Jobs Unlimited*. New York, N.Y.: The Macmillan Publishing Co.

Bolles, Richard N., *What Color Is Your Parachute*. Berkeley, California: Ten-Speed Press.

——————, *Where Do I Go With My Life*. Berkeley, California: Ten-Speed Press.

Bostwick, Burdette E., *Finding the Job You've Always Wanted*. New York, N.Y.: Wiley Interscience.

Duskiik, Richard H., *Your Career: How to Plan It, How to Manage It, How to Change It*. New York, N.Y.: New American Library.

Cohen, William A., *The Executives Guide to Finding A Superior Resume*. New York, N.Y.: American Management.

Corwen, Leonard, *Job Hunter's Handbook*. New York, N.Y.: Arco Books.

——————, *Your Future in Publishing*. New York, N.Y.: Rosen Press.

——————, *Your Resume—Key To A Better Job*. New York, N.Y.: Arco Publishing, Inc.

Figgins, Ross F., *Techniques of Job Search*. New York, N.Y.: Harper & Row.

Gainer, Harold N., and Stark, Sandra L., *Choice or Chance: A Guidebook For Career Planning*. New York, N.Y.: McGraw-Hill.

Gootnick, David, *Getting A Better Job*. New York, N.Y.: McGraw-Hill Book Co.

Gowdy, Eve, *Job Hunting With Employment Agencies*. Woodbury, N.Y.: Barron's.

179

Haldane, Bernard, *Career Satisfaction and Success*. New York, N.Y.: Amacom.

Irish, Richard K., *Go Hire Yourself An Employer*. New York, N.Y.: Doubleday & Co.

Jackson, Tom, *The Hidden Job Market*. New York, N.Y.: Times Books.

—————, *Guerilla Tactics in the Job Market*. New York, N.Y.: Bantam Books.

Lathrop, Richard, *Who's Hiring Who*. Berkeley, California: Ten-Speed Press.

McDonald, Stanleigh B., *Ten Weeks To A Better Job*. New York, N.Y.: Doubleday & Co.

Miner, Charles S., *How To Get An Executive Job After 40*. New York, N.Y.: The Macmillan Publishing Co.

Noer, David, *How To Beat The Employment Game*. Radnor, Pa.: Chilton Book Co.

Payne, Richard, *How to Get A Better Job Quicker*. New York, N.Y.: New American Library.

Pell, Arthur R., *The College Graduate's Guide to Job Finding*. New York, N.Y.: Monarch Press.

Resume Service Staff, *Resumes That Get Jobs*. New York, N.Y.: Arco Publishing, Inc.

Rust, Lee H., *Jobsearch: A Complete Guide to Successful Job Changing*. Saranac Lake, N.Y.: Amacom.

Strand, Stanley & Gruber, Edward C., *Resumes for Better Jobs*. New York, N.Y.: Monarch Press.

Thompson, Melvin R., *Why Should I Hire You?* New York, N.Y.: Harcourt, Brace, Jovanovich.

U.S. Government Printing Office, *Merchandising Your Job Talents*. Washington, D.C.

—————, *Occupational Outlook Handbook*. Washington, D.C.

Uris, Auren, *Action Guide for Executive Job Seekers and Employers*. New York, N.Y.: Arco Publishing, Inc.